BOYS
In Crisis

Slocumb, Paul D.
     Boys in Crisis, 4th edition
     (Previously titled *Hear Our Cry: Boys in Crisis*)
Paul D. Slocumb © 2004 xii, 170 pp. Revised 2015.
     Bibliography pp. 171–176
ISBN 13: 978-1-934583-45-6
ISBN 10: 1-934583-45-6

1. Education   2. Sociology   3. Title

Copy editing by Dan Shenk and Jesse Conrad

We gratefully acknowledge Jim Littlejohn, a long-time colleague of Dr. Slocumb,
for his work in updating the statistics and other items in chapters 1, 8, 9, and 10,
and the Appendix for this edition. Littlejohn worked closely with Dr. Slocumb
during his lifetime and is proud to carry his legacy forward as the most frequent
presenter of the Boys in Crisis workshops based on this book.

Paul D. Slocumb, Ed.D.

*This book is dedicated to
two significant men in my life.*

*One came before me:
my father, W.P. Slocumb.
He showed me a path.*

*The other one came behind me:
my son, Eric.
He shed light upon that path,
gave it meaning, and
showed me a road to self-discovery.
He has been my best teacher.*

Contents

Acknowledgments

A very special thank you goes to Dr. Ruby K. Payne, whose book *A Framework for Understanding Poverty* (1996, revised 2013) first wove the threads for a tapestry to make a difference in the lives of children from poverty throughout the world. Without her work and her support, this contribution would not exist.

Thank you, Dr. Janel Miller, for your guidance and commitment to others. You are a light at the end of a tunnel.

I give a special thank you to the countless boys and families of boys with whom I've had the opportunity to work as a teacher, campus administrator, and central office administrator. Your problems, concerns, and feelings were always heard and respected.

I offer a special thank you to the many teachers and administrators with whom I've had the privilege of working over the last 40 years for sharing your questions and experiences with me. You have all been my wonderful teachers.

Thank you, Dan Shenk, for always making the words and sentences clearer. You are a man of many words and talents.

To Donna Magee, who encouraged me to use the title of this book as the theme of my workshop on boys, thank you. Your support and insights are always welcomed and appreciated.

And, thank you, Jim D. Trammel, for being a true friend. Yes, two guys can be best friends for 40-plus years.

To my gifted and talented son, Eric, who has taught me more about manhood than he will ever know, and of whom I'm so proud for the man he has become, thank you.

Introduction

In my 40-plus years in the education profession, I have consistently worked with boys. That work also has been dominated by discipline issues. Having raised a son, I know the helplessness a parent feels when a boy is in pain — and the joy that comes when you realize you like the person in front of you, not because he's your son, but because of who he has become.

I have had the opportunity to work with many educators throughout the country on educating students from poverty and gifted students in poverty. In so doing, I have become acutely aware of the many discipline questions from teachers, with 95% of those questions regarding boys. As I have reviewed literature and reflected on my own experiences, I have become increasingly aware of how often the educational system falls short when it comes to reaching boys. In the United States, boys are in crisis.

More and more children are growing up without a dad. Family structures have changed. Affluent America is busy — and impoverished America is seeing the demise of the family unit. Sons are left alone with only the myths of a boy culture to guide them. If boys are to become the responsible fathers, husbands, businessmen, and community members they're capable of becoming, change must occur. The home and the school are where this begins.

In Chapter 11 of this book six case studies are presented. In these *true* scenarios six boys are introduced, along with significant others in their life at home and at school. You, the reader, are invited to help provide solutions for these boys, their families, and their schools. You are encouraged to first read the chapters preceding Chapter 11 in order to be better equipped to analyze the difficult situations — and the possible solutions. Perhaps in your own experience you will recognize one or more of the boys.

Bottom line: No boy should have to wait until his father is in his 60s to hear that he loves him. No student should have to wait until adulthood before he knows he's a person of worth, regardless of his background. No mother should have to feel that she must be both mother and father — or the translator of Dad's feelings and intentions toward the son. No boy should have to long for a relationship with his father like the one he has with his grandfather. No father should have to feel that he has to wait until his son becomes a man before he can show his son the nurturing side of himself. If we wait that long, it is likely too late. If we do, boys and young men will be lost in their own *emotional abyss*.

It is my devout hope that this work will further, or even begin, a necessary dialogue — and that educators and parents will hear the cry of our boys.

Chapter 1

The Crisis

"Without a sense
of right and wrong,
boundaries
don't exist."

—The Emotional Abyss
p. 27

If the current trend continues,
approximately two million Americans
will be under correctional supervision
within a ten-year period.
By 2020 the total probation, jail, prison,
and parole population
could reach 10,445,100.

West & Sabol, 2009

Chapter 1

The Crisis

On the surface, today's world is seemingly a man's world. Men make more money. They are taught from early in their lives that they can be anything they want to be. Compared with women, they have it made. So, what's the problem?

The issue is not what men have or don't have when compared with women. Both genders have their respective challenges and issues. The issue, ironically, is that we are now identifying stereotypical myths about men much in the same manner as feminists identify stereotypical myths about women.

Remember the outcries of women in the early years of the Equal Rights Amendment movement? Women all around were saying, "Whoa! Wait a minute. We aren't just homemakers and mothers. We're equals deserving of equal pay and advancement in the workplace." The women's movement went to great lengths to dispel these myths in order to change our culture and, more importantly, our perception of the roles women play in society. No such liberating movement has occurred for males.

It's now time for *males* to say, "Whoa! Wait a minute. We aren't just fighters, providers, and competitors who put winning above relationships." **Statistics on boys and men reflect the results of a society that has ignored the social and emotional life of boys.** To disregard the impact of these myths on young males is to put them in a decidedly weakened position to succeed personally, professionally, and emotionally — not to mention in terms of life expectancy: U.S. women on average outlive U.S. men by about five years.

To see the current trend, one need only refer to key statistics regarding the number of failed personal relationships, crimes committed by men and boys, juvenile males being tried as adults for adult crimes with greater frequency, and the larger and larger number of males who father children but don't parent.

At the end of 2001, about one in every 112 U.S. men and one in every 1,724 U.S. women were sentenced prisoners under the jurisdiction of state and federal authorities (Harrison & Beck, 2002). On December 31, 2013, the United States held an estimated 1,574,740 people in state and federal prisons (Carson, 2014). In 1990 the total was 1,148,702.

According to recent data from the Bureau of Justice Statistics, on December 31, 2013, the number of male prisoners compared with female prisoners under the jurisdiction of state or federal (not local) correctional authorities was significantly larger: 1,463,454 men compared with 111,287 women (Carson, 2014; see Appendix A). While the rate of incarceration for females is far lower than for males, it is increasing. Since 1990 the number of female defendants convicted of felonies in state courts has grown at more than twice the rate of increase in male defendants.

More than 2.7 million minor children have a parent who is currently incarcerated, and 10 million children have experienced parental incarceration. More than 11.4% of black children, 3.5% of Hispanic children, and 1.8% of white children have a parent in prison ("Children and Families," 2014). While growing up, 40% of parents in state prison reported living in a household that received public assistance, 14% reported living in a foster home, agency, or institution at some time during their youth, and 43% reported living with both parents most of the time. More than a third (34%) of parents in state prison reported that during their youth, their parents or guardians had abused alcohol or drugs ("Survey of Inmates," n.d.). Nearly 60% of women in state prisons had experienced physical or sexual abuse in the past.

These statistics are significant because:

- ◆ Male aggression contributes, at least in part, to female aggression.
- ◆ Many of the millions of minor children who have mothers under the supervision of justice system agencies also have a missing father.
- ◆ With mothers and fathers absent, the probability of children repeating the cycle of crime increases.

If appropriate interventions were implemented for young boys and young men, both male and female violence — and other forms of criminal behavior — would decrease.

These prison statistics are conservative figures because they are continually increasing. The Justice Department's Bureau of Justice Statistics projects that by 2020 the total number of adults in the United States who are in jail, prison, or on parole could total 10,445,100. Forty-three states have fewer than ten million people. If recent incarceration rates remain unchanged, an estimated one of every 15 people (6.6%) will serve time in prison during his or her lifetime. The chances of a person going to prison are higher for men (11.3%) than for women (1.8%). Blacks (18.6%) and Hispanics (10%) are more likely to go to prison than whites (3.4%). Among the nearly 1.6 million incarcerated offenders in 2013, an estimated 526,000 were black males, 454,100 were white males, and 314,600 were Hispanic males (Carson, 2014). Compounding this inequity is the probation rate. Fifty-five percent of adults on probation were white, 29% were black, and 13% were Hispanic. Forty-one percent of parolees were white, 38% were black, and 19% were Hispanic. The data suggest that whites are more likely to get probation than black males. The growing number of ex-prisoners means more people will have difficulty finding jobs because they have felony convictions. They are also more likely to have family or emotional problems.

School statistics are a predictor of later adult behaviors. Boys are three times more likely to be enrolled in special education than girls. Of students diagnosed with learning disabilities, 73% are boys. Of students diagnosed as emotionally disturbed, 76% are boys (Conlin, 2003). Boys are more likely to be retained in the same class and drop out of school, and they're four times more likely to be referred to a school psychologist (Kindlon & Thompson, 1999).

In every racial and ethnic group, females now outnumber males in the acquisition of college degrees. There are 133 females getting bachelor's degrees for every 100 males. This year the number is projected to reach 142 females for every 100 males, and 156 females per 100 males by 2020. The ratio of males to females at public universities is 43.6 to 56.4, and the ratio at private institutions is 40.7 to 59.3 (Borzelleca, 2012). Given current trends, school psychologist and coauthor of *Raising Cain* Dr. Michael Thompson states: "There's going to be a cold shower when the country realizes that women are completely dominating the numbers in professional schools. We can't have a country of women in white-collar jobs and men in blue-collar jobs. That's not going to be good for this society" (Kohn, 2003).

Judges commit boys to the juvenile justice system more often than they commit girls — even for the same offense. African-American boys are three times more likely to receive corporal punishment in school. Six white boys are physically paddled for every one white girl, and eight ethnically Asian boys are physically paddled for every one Asian girl. There's a greater likelihood that parents will paddle their boys than their girls. A survey of 8,000 men and 8,000 women interviewed in the National Violence Against Women Survey showed that men were significantly more likely than women to have experienced physical abuse as children (Thompson, Kingree, & Desai, 2004).

Boys commit 95% of juvenile homicides. Boys are the perpetrators in four out of five crimes that end up in juvenile court. Boys under the age of 18 are responsible for close to one-fifth of the violent crime in the United States. The suicide rate for males between the ages of 15 and 24 is significantly higher than it is for females in the same age range.

Boys dominate teachers' and administrators' time, as well as consume more of the school's time by considerably outnumbering girls in the following areas:

- Being referred to the office for discipline
- Lagging behind in reading and writing
- Being suspended from school
- Qualifying for special education services
- Not being promoted to the next grade level
- Dropping out of school
- Committing crimes at school

The reasons for this collective disparity are as complex as the boys are individually. This disparity results in boys being unfulfilled as men who are disconnected emotionally and from their responsibilities to their families, communities, and workplaces.

The factors and circumstances that increase the probability that boys will have difficulty in school include the following:

1. As boys have slipped in their academic performance, there has been little of the public outcry that went up for girls in the 1960s and 1970s, especially among feminist groups.

2. More fathers attend athletic events to watch their sons play sports than attend PTA or PTO meetings. The unspoken message to boys is that physical prowess is valued more than mental prowess.

3. There is a shortage of male teachers.

4. Classrooms reward on-task behavior, sitting still, concentrating, and focusing on pencil/paper tasks. This makes for girl-friendly classrooms and boy-unfriendly classrooms.

5. High-spirited, competitive boys are generally viewed as having behavior problems.

6. Boys are more likely to tease other boys who embrace academics. Boys often perceive academics as a feminine or "wimpy" pursuit, while sports are seen as manly.

7. In spite of the gains females have made academically and in the job market, they still don't receive pay equal to that of their male co-workers. The message for young boys is that they'll still make more money than their female counterparts, and that this is largely unrelated to academic performance.

8. Certain jobs are still stereotyped as male or female jobs. Ask a 14-year-old boy if he wants to be a nurse or a flight attendant when he grows up and note the response of his peers, as well as that of his dad.

9. Many parents, teachers, and law enforcement officials assume that when there's trouble, the perpetrator is a boy.

10. Parents and educators lack an understanding of the social, emotional, and neurological differences between males and females and, as a result,

seldom accommodate these differences. This leads to lowered self-esteem in many young boys who see themselves as incapable, unlovable, and inefficient learners.

11. The image of males in the media shows violence as a means for solving differences; male-on-male violence is a prevalent theme of most action movies.

12. Boys in poverty are frequently dependent on single moms or grandmothers. These are often the only close-to-home role models a boy has.

13. Many fathers lack the emotional vocabulary and skills necessary to help their sons through their emotional pain.

The chapters that follow explore the factors that place boys in this crisis situation. Every boy who marries and doesn't become a responsible adult, parent, spouse, or employee places a family in jeopardy, and those around him suffer the loss of yet another male who has failed to connect to his goodness and potential as a human being. Every father who doesn't become emotionally engaged with his family increases the likelihood that his children will be lost to crime, drugs, alcohol, and other self-destructive behaviors. Correspondingly, every child who is left to be raised by a single mother with a limited education is more likely to become a member of a generation caught up in the cycle of poverty, especially if that single mom lacks a high school diploma. The statistics are prophetic.

U.S. Census data show that single women who lack a high school diploma have more than a 50% chance of living below the poverty line.

Another key factor is the discrepancy in pay for females versus that of males. Though females have made gains in equal employment opportunities, equal pay has not become a reality in the workplace. For a female to come close to making equal pay to a male requires that she achieve two educational levels higher than he.

A female without a high school diploma almost guarantees that her children will live in poverty — if not permanently, at least temporarily. Placing an employed male in the home greatly reduces that probability. With a current divorce rate of 50% or greater, boys must be educated about the significance of their role in the lives of the children they will someday father. Their sexual conquests must be replaced with a sexual conscience and sense of responsibility. Child-support checks from prison will only imprison the children left behind.

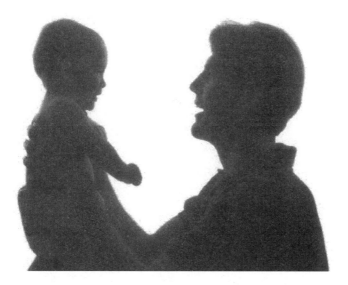

Dads who stay involved in the lives of their sons produce young men who perform better in school and in personal relationships. Emotionally healthy, secure dads increase the probability that their sons also will be emotionally healthy, productive adults.

Chapter 2

The Brains Behind the Man

"He will refuse
to perform academically
because it isn't cool to be smart.
He can't handle
the rejection of his peers."

—The Emotional Abyss
p. 27

On a scale of 0 to 500,
the average reading score for
fourth-grade girls in 2000 was 222
compared with boys at 212.

Conlin, 2003

Chapter 2

The Brains Behind the Man

Why can't they sit still? Why do they always have to win? Why are they so stubborn? Why are they so argumentative? Why do they have to pretend that nothing is wrong? Why won't he stop and ask for directions? He never talks to me; he won't let me in. Why can't my son express his feelings like my daughter does? Why do they always have to be so tough? Why?

It's "that guy thing!"

"That guy thing" is really that brain thing. The male brain is configured differently from the female brain, and these differences are rarely taken into account in personal relationships, parenting, or in the classroom. The hormonal differences that affect the brain — and ultimately behavior — begin in the womb around the sixth week after conception.

Male and female fetuses look the same during the first six weeks of life — and then things change dramatically. Around the sixth week, the Y chromosome triggers the testosterone, which causes the testicles to drop in males. This hormone has a significant impact on the brain and the subsequent physical development of boys (Baron-Cohen, Lutchmaya, & Knickmeyer, 2004). Boys eventually have about 20 times as much testosterone as girls, and together with other hormones, testosterone contributes to the very developmental trajectory of boys.

The embryonic brain takes some time before it begins to acquire a sexual identity. If the embryo is a female physically, nothing very dramatic happens to the brain. The natural template of the brain seems to be female (Moir & Jessel, 1992). This natural template is changed radically, however, if the gender is a male. For boys, hormones affect male brain patterns. Embryonic boy babies are exposed to large doses of male hormones during brain formation. This surge of male hormones becomes dramatic during two key times in a boy's life:

- Six weeks after conception, when the brain is beginning to take shape.
- During adolescence, when his sexuality is defined.

The hormones necessary to develop the male sex organs may not be able to produce enough additional male hormones to push the brain into the male pattern. The brain may say "female" but be put in a "male" body. The female who is exposed to doses of male hormones may result in a female body with a "male" brain. The dosage amount of hormones affects the fetus and produces a variety of combinations that later affect behavior patterns in both males and females.

According to Dr. Anne Moir and David Jessel (1992), such combinations can produce male bodies with male brains, male bodies with female brains, female bodies with male brains, or female bodies with female brains. Stereotyping males and females on the basis of overt behavior patterns reinforces myths about both males and females. For children, these stereotypes of males and females often result in derogatory comments from peers ("She's a tomboy"; "he's a sissy"), leaving lasting, negative emotional effects. What is needed is a tolerance for a range of behavior and thinking patterns that can appear in both males and females because of the hardwiring of the brain, as well as early influences in childhood. The homosexual/heterosexual nature versus nurture controversy will be left to the medical professionals who are still debating the issue.

As indicated, hormones produce some differences in the hardwiring of the male brain. These differences dictate many of the behaviors observed in males. Some of these hormonal factors begin to have less of an impact on male behavior after the age of 35, when testosterone levels start declining rather precipitously. Though the hardwiring is present in the male brain, males can learn alternative behaviors. It should be noted, however, that these learned behaviors are contrary to the original wiring of the male brain.

Think of the brain as a house with many rooms. The male house has a number of rooms, each of which has a special purpose; the female brain, on the other hand, has rooms that are multipurpose. Males are hardwired to be literal and objective. They want proof, proof, and more proof. The literal, objective male brain is highly specialized, making it more difficult for males to access the various rooms in their house. It's as if their brains are singular in focus and purpose. The male must make a conscious choice and deliberately think about accessing parts of his brain. For males, feelings are housed in a special room, one that is often locked. When a male has to stop and think how he feels about a situation, he must first take time to find the key that will unlock this special room.

Females, on the other hand, are hardwired to be subjective and intuitive. Females use their intuition. While the male brain is very specialized, the female brain is much more integrated. The female accesses different parts of her brain much more readily than does the male. For the female, feelings are an integral part of every room of the house. There are no locked rooms in the female brain.

Michael Gurian, author of ***Boys and Girls Learn Differently*** (2001), describes males as deductive thinkers, whereas girls tend to be inductive. Boys begin with the general and then apply it to a specific situation. Girls look at the examples, build the generalizations, and derive theories from them. In general, boys tend to be compulsive, enjoy problem solving, and are more competitive than girls.

When teachers put boys in a small group for a learning experience, boys will spend much of their time trying to determine who is going to be the leader.

Small-group work isn't something most boys would choose. Boys do, however, migrate to larger groups, such as athletic teams, special-interest clubs, and sporting events as a spectator. Because boys tend to be competitive, most are slower to form bonds for fear they'll have to compete with and "beat" their best friend. Because boys are competitive, they're hardwired in the brain not to seek help. Seeking help shows weakness and makes one vulnerable. It also can mean the other person "wins."

Girls, on the other hand, gravitate toward small-group activity. Because, as a gender group, they're less competitive, they often work well with others in a spirit of cooperation. Girls are more inclined than boys to call attention to personal distress because they don't have as much of a need to "do it myself." This lower level of competitiveness allows girls to form friendships more easily than boys. It also allows them to seek the help of others, making them effective leaders who work cooperatively with diverse opinions and personalities.

The differences in language acquisition and the use of language are probably two of the most significant factors that impede boys academically and socially. The first segment of the male brain to develop is the part that governs spatial abilities. The last portion to develop is language. The opposite occurs in females. The corpus callosum, a bridge located in the front of the brain, is smaller in males than in females. As a result, the crossover between the left and right hemispheres of the brain takes longer for the male. Because of this, most females are better at multitasking than are most males. Males tend to do one thing at a time, getting closure to that task, then moving on to the next task. The male brain is highly specialized; most males tend to access each area one at a time as needed.

Boys tend to relate to diagrams and abstractions better than information dealing with words. Communicating thoughts, feelings, and ideas requires hard, precise language. Boys tend to be logical and more driven to solve problems. Girls use more words when they talk. They read more, write more, and develop their verbal skills a year or more before boys do. Drs. Dan Kindlon and Michael Thompson (1999) contend that this difference in language development is so pronounced that, at least from the academic standpoint, most boys would be better served in school if as 8-year-olds they were grouped with 6-year-old girls for reading and writing instruction. By third grade, however, boys do start making strides to close the gap in language development between them and girls. But because of the brain differences, males as a gender group never completely catch up with females in the language arena.

The most crucial time for most boys in the learning process is kindergarten, first grade, and second grade. When boys struggle with reading and writing in those early years, they often form negative attitudes about reading and writing, which in turn sets the stage for negative attitudes about learning throughout their educational journeys. Boys have a difficult time processing language when they are constantly being bombarded by words. Eighty percent of the teacher workforce in American schools is female, and as a gender group they use too many words for most boys. When boys are bombarded by many words, the male brain tends to go into a rest state. The result is the blank stare that many teachers and parents see on the faces of their boys. That blank stare (daydreaming, glazing over, tuning out) is often described, by the time boys reach third grade, as attention deficit disorder (ADD). What is happening biologically is that the male brain has to regroup. It's like the computer that doesn't have enough RAM (random access memory), and the computer locks up. Males as a gender group want the bottom line. Most of them really don't want to hear all the peripheral details. How many times has a husband said to his wife, "Is there a point to this?"

The female's facility with language allows girls to process emotive data much more quickly than males. They also tend to be more sensory, and their use of language is more concrete rather than abstract. They tend to trust their intuition about other people. Since the corpus callosum is larger in females, they can process more cross-talk between the two hemispheres of

the brain. The male takes in far less information concurrently. Males tend not to trust their intuition about a person's character. Rather, they look for logical conclusions based on concrete evidence. Females trust their intuitive self and require less evidence before drawing conclusions. Females absorb explanations more quickly.

Certainly there are exceptions to these generalizations, but as gender groups, the natures of males and females are quite different. The differences in male and female brain configurations manifest themselves in schools, family relationships, and social relationships. Through social interaction, innate differences can be changed in both males and females. Genetic tendencies do not have to be the fate of either gender. Females have shown this through their competitiveness with males in the workplace, as well as their increasingly intense competition in sports. Environmental and social influences can help males become far more (and deeper) than competitive beings who must win. The largest step, however, is for the male to become emotionally connected to himself. To achieve this, boys must overcome one major difference between themselves and girls — a lack of facility with language to articulate thoughts, feelings, and ideas.

This lack of language sets up most males to be largely disconnected emotionally. Without words (without a nuanced vocabulary), males have great difficulty negotiating their position in school and the world. The main alternative means of communication is nonverbal action, often taking the form of violence or negative or self-destructive behaviors. The end result for many boys is spending more time in the principal's office than in the classroom — and suffering feelings of frustration for which they have no words.

CREATING A MORE BOY-FRIENDLY CLASSROO

- In the primary grades, consider having all-boy reading groups. Boys are less likely to compare their reading ability with girls if they are not competing with them.

- When giving boys explanations, try to get to the bottom line. Think in terms of bulleted items or lists.

- Appeal to the spatial and graphic abilities of boys. Instead of a step sheet that is in narrative form, put it in a flowchart. Step 1 might be in a square with an arrow to Step 2 that is in a circle, etc.

- Don't shy away from inquiry lessons and Socratic questioning, but when a boy appears to be getting frustrated, be prepared to give him a generalization, then ask him to find the examples. Being a deductive thinker is his strength.

- When a boy is frustrated with high levels of anxiety, try to give him a private place to process — and offer him water to drink. When levels of anxiety increase, cortisol (a stress hormone) is released in the brain. The brain is 75% water. Drinking water allows the cortisol to be diluted, thus lowering levels of anxiety. The effect of consuming water takes effect in about five minutes. If water is room temperature, a person can wait longer before having to go to the restroom; cold water moves through the body faster.

- When a boy needs think time, a rocking chair can be useful (particularly in the primary grades, counselor's office, or the principal's office). The rocking chair provides the boy an opportunity to experience movement. However, you may need to help some boys realize that the rocking chair is not a launching pad!

- The retina of the male eye is different from the female. Young girls tend to use bright colors, including pastels, in their drawings. They draw mommies and daddies, babies, puppies, houses, flowers, and sunshine. Boys tend to favor black, brown, gray, and navy blue, with a splash of "blood" thrown in. They draw dragons, daggers, trucks, and monsters. This is not a pathology and is no cause for concern.

- There's a 15% greater blood flow in the female brain than in the male brain. This contributes to the rest state that many males experience when they're being bombarded by words. When boys begin to have that blank stare in a classroom, move closer to the boy (proximity), do a touch on the shoulder, have him physically do something, or stop and ask the boy a question. This will help the boy shift from input mode to output mode.

- The inner ear of males is different from that of females. Many boys do not hear certain sounds. If you are a soft-spoken teacher, consider moving the boys in your classroom closer to the front of the room. Boys are sometimes accused of yelling when they're really just talking louder. Leonard Sax's book *Why Gender Matters* is an excellent resource on this.

- Because the corpus callosum is 25% larger in the female brain than in the male brain, females tend to be much better at multitasking. Males generally prefer doing one thing at a time. When attempting to get boys to shift from one activity to another, consider using a timer. Set the timer and say, "Try to get to a stopping point before the timer goes off." Most boys will compete with the clock because they tend to be highly competitive.

- Use action verbs and very descriptive adjectives when communicating emotions or expectations with boys. If you say to a boy, "When you do that, it really upsets me," most boys won't understand what you mean. But if you say, "When you do that, it makes me really angry," he will understand what you mean. Use hard language with boys. "Behave" has little meaning. Be specific and descriptive.

- For boys who need to move, try to allow them to have an area in which to move. Place some desks at the back of the room and put masking tape on the floor. Say to the boys: "If you need to move while reading, writing, etc., you can sit at that desk and get up as long as you stay within the taped-off area." Most boys can move in this way without disturbing others.

- Allow boys more physical space. As noted previously, boys move and need space in which to move. To minimize disciplinary problems in the primary grades, allow boys space that comprises twice their body width. When children are forming a big circle on the floor, make the circle bigger. Boys will be on their knees, on their bottom, feet to left and then to the right. Give them the space in which to do that. Masking tape on the floor can be an effective way for boys to identify their personal boundary. In classrooms in which flat-topped desks are used to form groups of four, pull the desks back about six inches. It will give boys the feeling of more space.

- Provide boys reading material that is more action-centered. Audio books, graphic books, how-to books, sports, cars, and adventure appeal to many boys.

- Create learning games that require competition. Again, as noted above, most boys are motivated by competition and problem solving.

- To promote writing, allow boys to draw pictures of what they want to say. Many boys love to doodle. Use that to your advantage. It can be a pre-writing activity that motivates boys. Draw pictures of vocabulary words. The brain has a limited ability to remember words, but it has an almost unlimited capacity to remember pictures.

- When praising boys orally, try to do so privately. Group praise can be done with high-fives or a "thumbs-up." Giving a boy verbal praise in front of his peers may set him up for teasing ("Ahh, teacher's pet" or "kissing up").

- Avoid visually cluttered walls. When many things are mounted on a classroom wall, it can be overstimulating for many boys, especially if primary colors dominate the room. Put things in an orderly fashion. Student work can be placed in areas as though it were in a picture frame. Create white space, then create another area of display. Because spatial ability is a strength in the male brain, boys try to figure out patterns, and it can be very distracting when things are cluttered. Setting a tri-fold on each student's desk also can be a way of helping students — boys in particular — concentrate.

- ◆ Allow boys to play with Nerf balls while reading.

- ◆ Having boys work in pairs rather than larger small groups minimizes competition among boys.

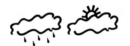

Chapter 3

I Dunno. I'm Fine!

"Without an emotional language,
empathy does not exist."

—The Emotional Abyss
p. 27

Boys far outnumber girls in special education.

Diagnosed as emotionally disturbed:
    Boys: 73%
    Girls: 27%

Secondary students in special education:
    Boys: 76%
    Girls: 24%

Conlin, 2003

Chapter 3

I Dunno.
I'm Fine!

T he lack of words, the driving need to compete, the need to be in motion, and the inability to articulate feelings set boys up to have difficulty academically, socially, and emotionally. In their struggle to protect themselves from these swirling conflicts, many boys turn their feelings inward and retreat to their room.

Males have been in their room for a very long time. A room can be any place where a guy doesn't have to share his feelings with the rest of the world. Historically, males have been warriors. They leave home and sail the high seas and explore faraway places. They roam. They are heroes who love adventure. Odysseus leaves his son Telemachus behind for 25 years. Columbus leaves his family to discover new lands. Lewis and Clark open new trails for others to follow. No one talks about the families these men left behind. More importantly, they were not seen as dead-beat dads.

Today, the male still is expected to be the warrior, but it's in the workplace. He must make that sale at all costs. He is expected to do whatever it takes in order to provide for his family.

It gets no better for men in the media. The male is the butt of the jokes in most TV situation comedies; the rational thinker in most sitcoms is a female. In action

25

movies, the collision between fantasy and reality is even more striking. Males destroy their enemy. Males have superhuman strength. No matter how many cars and buildings are blown up, or how many people attack him, our hero survives!

The boy in school tries to live up to this same masculine image. The star athlete is expected to keep playing, regardless of pain or injury. He must push himself to win at all cost. When the word *hurt* surfaces, he turns the pain and shame inward to save face. To do anything else would make him weak in the eyes of other males. And warriors simply are not weak!

These models are insufficient today. Today's Lewis and Clark are blazing new trails in space, doing medical research, protecting the environment, and solving social problems. Modern man must function as a productive team member in the workplace, in the family, and in his community. He must have the skills and attitudes necessary to be a strong, authentic person who knows how to develop and maintain strong, affectionate relationships with spouses, children, parents, co-workers, neighbors, and friends. Even men who choose jobs that require physical confrontations, such as law enforcement and the military, still need to function within families and communities. To do this, boys must develop a facility with language that allows them not only to read and write, but also to develop an emotional vocabulary. Without this, boys run the risk of spiraling downward into an ***emotional abyss***. The absence of an emotional vocabulary is a key catalyst for the emotional abyss.

THE EMOTIONAL ABYSS

◆ Without an emotional language, empathy does not exist.

◆ Without empathy, conscience can't develop.

◆ Without a conscience, there is little sense of right and wrong.

◆ Without a sense of right and wrong, boundaries don't exist.

◆ Without boundaries, it's very difficult to articulate a personal code of ethics or have a sense of integrity.

◆ Without ethics and integrity, words are limited.

◆ Frustration turns to anger, and anger turns to rage. The result is raw, misdirected energy with few words.

$$ The Price $$

◆ He will bully those who are different and vulnerable. His weapons are words, fists, and guns.

◆ He will vandalize and abuse his surroundings; the rules don't apply to him. His environment triggers anger and self-hatred.

◆ He will refuse to perform academically because it isn't cool to be smart. He can't handle the rejection of his peers.

◆ He will cheat his employer by reporting expenses he did not incur, stealing the hammer he needs at home, calling in sick when he wants a day off, and blaming others for his mistakes. Everyone owes him.

◆ He will use manipulative and deceitful practices in the corporate world in order to win, no matter the cost to others.

◆ He will remain disconnected emotionally from his wife and children, and his relationships will disintegrate or simply go unfulfilled. The void remains.

Schools, parents, and the workplace must be willing to show boys that there's more than one way to be a guy. Women now know that their gender doesn't determine the kind of work they can do. Males must learn that there's more than one road to masculinity. It begins by developing an emotional honesty with oneself. To do this, however, requires language.

Without the words to express their thoughts, ideas, and especially feelings, boys are left to express themselves through behavior. Those behaviors often become the sources of criticism, even sanctions. Boys often have difficulty in the following types of situations and circumstances:

- ◆ A quick response to an emotional issue is expected, allowing little time for processing.

- ◆ Hormonal changes during adolescence impact the brain, making the boy want to move, while parents and teachers are saying "sit still." The simultaneous presence of physical urges and social expectations creates conflict.

- ◆ Difficulty learning to read causes some boys to feel stupid in front of others.

- ◆ Peers or adults taunt boys about their physical appearance or their inability to perform well.

- ◆ Teachers (and other adults) sometimes use sarcasm to discipline or motivate boys.

- ◆ Boys imitate male-on-male violence seen in the media as a way of solving problems. This often results in punishment.

- ◆ Parents and educators don't establish an emotional safety zone in which a boy can talk without being judged: "C'mon, grow up. Take it like a man!"

- ◆ Boys are prescribed medication because they're incapable of controlling their behavior. They need to be "fixed" with a pill or some physical punishment.

- ◆ Parents and educators use their harsh "parenting voice" to scold and reprimand boys, resulting in increased pain and anger rather than resolution.

To be successful in adult relationships, boys must replace competitiveness with empathy, negotiation, and compromise (Pollack, 1998). Boys must become more caring, dependent, and vulnerable. To achieve this, the mindset that a boy needs to be a rugged individualist — and suffer alone and in silence — must be replaced with words. To free boys from enduring a pattern of fear and loneliness, an emotional vocabulary must be developed.

LACK OF LANGUAGE

Your son comes home from school. "Matt, how was your day?" "Fine," he responds. "You look a little upset." "No, Mom. I'm fine," he replies. "Are you sure you don't want to talk about it?" "No, Mom, I'm fine. Do you have to keep bugging me?" Off he goes to his room and closes the door.

> **Matt tucks his feelings away, deep inside himself. He suffers alone. He is alone physically and emotionally.**

Your daughter comes home from school. "Hi, Sara, how was your day?" "Momma, you won't believe what they did to me on the bus!" As she begins to cry and tell her story, the mother comforts her daughter, showing the sensitivity and empathy of a caring mom.

> **Sara expresses her feelings, which in turn are accepted, nurtured, and validated — both physically and emotionally.**

Most parents who have raised a son and a daughter can relate to the silence of boys and the verbosity of girls. One of the key myths for boys is that they must keep their emotions in check — and maintain that stiff upper lip. To acknowledge pain and not be able to deal with problems alone means, at least to them, that they're weak. To be a heroic warrior like your forefathers requires suffering in silence. Without the words to express the pain, and without the permission to express the pain, the pain can turn to anger, and the anger ultimately can turn to rage.

This lack of language begins biologically. If that lack isn't counteracted with appropriate nurturing in the preschool years, the biological inclination lingers. As stated in Chapter 2, boys as a group develop language at a slower pace than girls. They tend to avoid words and instead show their emotions through action. Dr. William Pollack (1998) describes boys as action-oriented. They often experience what he calls a "timed silence syndrome." When the emotions hit, they have to go to their room for processing time.

The male brain doesn't allow boys the quick processing time girls tend to experience. In a study of boys' and girls' processing of emotive data, boys were found to take as much as five hours longer to process emotive data than girls, who tend to deal with such data almost immediately. Boys typically don't have the emotional vocabulary of girls, and they aren't nurtured to be in touch with their feelings in the ways most girls are.

Not having the words, boys often express their emotions through anger and aggression. A crying baby has no words. Crying becomes the expression of the feelings the baby is experiencing. As a toddler, the lack of words may manifest itself as a temper tantrum. During adolescence, the absence of words is frequently called an "attitude." *An "attitude" in most cases stems from a dearth of words. It's a non-verbal means of expressing one's feelings, thoughts, and ideas.* Non-verbal communication is often more powerful than words. One may forget someone's words, but the "attitude" is remembered. "If only he would change his attitude," lament teachers, parents, and school administrators. Words may not be understood by some, but the non-verbal "attitude" is a universal language, no matter where one lives or what language is spoken.

Boys from Poverty — the Double Whammy!

For boys from poverty, anger and aggression can become even more intense. Growing up in an environment that is concrete, emotional, and sensory-based, boys in poverty aren't exposed to language in the same way as middle-class boys. With limited language, a person doesn't have the tools necessary to manipulate and negotiate his/her position in the world. To develop that ability, an abstract structure must be built in the mind. Language and experience build that structure (Payne, 2013). Most adults mediate their children. In *Understanding Learning* (2002b), Dr. Ruby K. Payne writes: "The mediation of the mind happens when an individual is taught the *what,* the *why,* and the *how*" [emphasis added] (p. 10). She uses the following example to illustrate this process.

- ◆ "'Don't cross the street without looking' (what).
- ◆ "'You could be killed' (why).
- ◆ "'Look both ways twice before you cross the street' (how)" (p. 7).

In poverty this process is typically lacking. A study by Drs. Betty Hart and Todd Risley (1995) shows a high correlation between the levels of language development in young children and the economic level of the parents. They also found a high correlation between the children's level of language and the mother's level of education — the higher her educational level, the more advanced the child's facility with language. In a study of preschool children between the ages of 6 months and 36 months, Hart and Risley found a significant difference in both the quantity and quality of the language spoken to young children.

DIFFERENCES IN WELFARE, WORKING-CLASS, AND PROFESSIONAL-CLASS PRESCHOOLERS' LANGUAGE EXPERIENCE

Social Group	Number of Words Heard per Hour	Estimated Number of Words Heard per Week	Words of Encouragement versus Discouragement per Week
Welfare children	616	62,000	500 vs. 1,100
Working-class children	1,251	125,000	1,200 vs. 700
Professional-class children	2,153	215,000	3,200 vs. 500

Hart and Risley, 1995

Words of discouragement are:

- ◆ Don't!
- ◆ Quit!
- ◆ Stop it!
- ◆ Move over!
- ◆ Shut up!
- ◆ Be quiet!
- ◆ I'm gonna slap you!

All of these tell the **what.** They don't include the **how** or the **why.** Without all three, the child doesn't learn cause and effect. That pattern isn't recorded in the brain. All of these words are sensory, emotional, and concrete. They're also words of aggression. Unfortunately, students often experience similar language in the classroom:

- ◆ Sit down!
- ◆ Be quiet!
- ◆ Get busy!
- ◆ Stop talking!
- ◆ Get to work!
- ◆ Stop clowning around!
- ◆ Go to the office!

Dr. Carolyn Weiner, in **Preparing for Success** (2001), explores the reasons young children from poverty backgrounds don't do as well in school as middle-income children. Her research focuses on language acquisition and differences between what the children come to school with versus what the school expects. Weiner asserts that children have a "Language Information Structure" (LIS), and the classroom presents a "Language Information Load" (LIL). Children from poverty typically come to school at a much lower level of language proficiency than middle-class children. Weiner maintains that the degree of alignment between the child's LIS and the school's LIL directly impacts learning. Her conclusions include:

When the LIL exceeds the LIS:

- ◆ Content learning is impaired.
- ◆ The level of the LIS slowly increases.

When the LIL is less than the LIS:

- ◆ Content learning is easier.
- ◆ Specific vocabulary may increase.
- ◆ The level of the LIS does not increase.

When the LIL equals the LIS:

- ◆ Content learning is maximized.
- ◆ The level of the LIS rapidly increases.

Weiner, 2001, p. 5

> THE UNPREDICTABLE OFTEN BECOMES THE PREDICTABLE.

For boys from poverty, both environment and biology work against them in the school environment. The predictable difficulties these boys will have in school increase the probability that inappropriate behavior will soon become the focus of educators and parents. When boys don't make satisfactory progress in the primary grades, they often become convinced they're dumb, they can't learn, and they're bad. The shame connected to boys' inability to please the teacher academically *and* socially sets the stage for a painful journey, grade level after grade level.

The fact that a boy doesn't have the words to talk about the feelings triggered by this academic challenge compounds the emotional pain at a very young age. For this to change, schools must place a high priority on language acquisition for young children — particularly boys. When the assumption is that all children are ready to begin at the same level, the gap between poverty students and middle-income children widens. When the language "load" of the curriculum requires that boys from poverty use language that is beyond the language structure they have in their brain, learning will be impaired.

WORDS: KEYS OF THE MIND

The lack of words imprisons the mind. Without the words, one cannot achieve metacognition, to think about one's thinking. Payne (2010) distinguishes the mind from the brain: what is learned in the environment versus what one inherits genetically. She states: "…[M]ore importantly, it is the abstract replication/representation of external reality" (p. 199). Students from poverty tend not to develop that abstract (mental) structure because of the concrete, sensory, and emotional nature of poverty.

Patty Duke's portrayal of Helen Keller in the movie classic "The Miracle Worker" is an excellent example of what happens when one doesn't have language. Without the words to label things, ideas, and emotions, the void may well be filled with anger and aggression. The mind is literally trapped in darkness. When Helen Keller finally figured out that finger signs represented objects, her mind was unlocked and began absorbing everything in the environment. Words unlock the mind; they are the key.

Martin Joos (1967) found that all languages have five registers. Payne (2013) describes these five registers as:

Register	Descriptor
Frozen	Language that is always the same: Lord's Prayer, wedding vows, etc. It is predictable.
Formal	The standard sentence syntax and word choice of the business and school communities. Sentence syntax is complete, and word choice is specific.
Consultative	Formal register when used in conversation. Discourse pattern is not quite as direct as formal register.
Casual	Language between friends. Normal conversational vocabulary is limited to 400 to 800 words. Word choice is general and not specific. Conversation is dependent upon non-verbal assists. Sentence syntax is often incomplete.
Intimate	Language between lovers or twins. Language of sexual harassment.

Payne, 2013, p. 31

Students from poverty typically don't have access to formal register at home. Casual register condenses language. Standard sentence syntax is reduced to a few words and is assisted through the use of non-verbal body language. As noted earlier, the use of the body to communicate is often referred to as an "attitude." Without standard sentence syntax and word choice, students cannot manipulate and negotiate their position in the world. For boys hardwired to be physically active (and because language isn't typically an innate strength), casual register appears to be a natural fit. Without the intervention of adults who insist on the use of words and standard sentence syntax, boys end up with a communication system that utilizes few words. For boys from poverty who usually aren't exposed to formal register during their preschool years, casual register is almost inevitable. They're also virtually assured of not learning formal register, unless there's mediation and intervention.

NEGOTIATING POWER AND POSITION IN SCHOOL

What does this look like in school? In a 7th-grade Social Studies class, the teacher has the students working in small groups. She realizes she needs an atlas from the library. Johnny, a young man from poverty, is asked to go to the library, ask the librarian for an atlas, and hurry right back. Being from poverty, Johnny cannot just walk quietly to the door and do as requested. He has to make a statement to his peers that he is the chosen one. His declaration begins with "the walk." He gives some of his buddies a high-five as he walks by, does a guy-punch on the bicep of another one of his buddies, and knocks the books off another guy's desk, probably someone he has been picking on in the hall. Finally, he gets to the door, and everyone knows he is the chosen one.

He gets out into the hallway where a teacher is on hall duty. "Young man, I need to see your hall pass." "Don't got one," he responds. "Well, you can't be in the hall without a hall pass. You need to go back to your class." "Can't," he declares. "What do you mean you can't? Where do you think you're going?" "Library," he answers confidently. "Well, you can't go to the library without a hall pass." "Got to. My teacher tol' me," he retorts. Johnny begins to walk off. The teacher calls him back. Johnny mumbles, "This sucks." The teacher asks, "What did you say?" He answers her question: "This sucks!" Johnny soon lands in the principal's office. The charges:

- ✓ No hall pass
- ✓ Insubordinate
- ✓ Defying authority
- ✓ Inappropriate language

Johnny is in big trouble and doesn't have the words or processing time to explain to the principal what happened. He burns with anger. He's convinced this isn't fair and that teachers and principals don't like him.

The same scenario with a middle-class student who does have language comes out quite differently. Billy, a middle-class student, is asked to go the library, get an atlas, and hurry right back. Billy, unlike Johnny, leaves the room quietly, with purpose, and disturbs no one.

He gets into the hallway and is asked by the teacher on duty for his hall pass. Billy responds, "I'm sorry, Mrs. Jones didn't give me one. She asked me to go the library and get an atlas and hurry right back. I guess she was just real busy and forgot. Do you want me to go back to class and get a hall pass, or may I go on to the library and get the atlas for Mrs. Jones?" The teacher on duty leans over, pats Billy on the shoulder, and says, "Well, Honey, that's OK this time. You hurry on to the library and get that atlas and get back to class. No dillydallying."

What is the difference? Both boys have broken the same school rule. One ends up in the office, while the other gets a pat on the back. The difference is language, having the words to negotiate and manipulate one's position in the world. If Johnny is African-American or Hispanic and Billy is white, Johnny thinks the difference is race. The color of one's skin is concrete; language is abstract. Johnny knows what happened to him when he didn't have a hall pass, and he knows what happened to Billy. He knows what color his skin is and what color Billy's skin is. He doesn't know anything about this language stuff. And how do school officials describe Johnny's behavior? "Johnny has a bad attitude! He's trouble!"

Dave Pelzer is the author of the autobiographical trilogy *A Child Called "It"* (1995), *The Lost Boy* (1997), and *A Man Named Dave* (1999). When he was placed in foster care, Pelzer was the third-worst child abuse case in California history. In the second book of the series, young Dave struggles to survive in the foster system. While in one of his several foster families, Dave is trying to adjust to his new school and trying to fit in. John is a member of a gang, and Dave is asked to join, but before doing so there are some things he must do. After John has a confrontation with his teacher, Mr. Smith, John solicits Dave's help in exchange for becoming a member of the gang. John decides to burn Mr. Smith's classroom. John starts the fire, and Dave ends up trying to extinguish it while John runs from the scene of the crime. A fellow student sees Dave and reports that Dave started the fire.

Dave ends up declaring "I didn't do it!" to his principal and to his foster parents. That's as far as Dave's words and facility with language can take him in trying to save himself. He ends up serving time in juvenile detention, afraid and lacking the words to explain what really happened. He becomes the victim of his lack of facility with language, doing time for a crime he didn't commit. His fear, his emotions, and his inexperience are as real and confusing as his lack of language.

> **Without a facility with language, boys cannot articulate statements that call for cause-and-effect relationships. Without cause and effect, boys have little concept of consequences, either negative or positive. Without the words to articulate cause-and-effect relationships and an understanding of consequences, boys don't develop an emotional literacy and the corresponding conscience. Empathy cannot exist. Emotions are acted out.**
>
> **He is entering the *emotional abyss*.**

Chapter 4

Pain, Anger, and Rage

> " ... anger turns to rage.
> The result is raw, misdirected energy
> with few words."

—The Emotional Abyss
p. 27

Twelfth-grade girls outnumber boys in all areas of extracurricular activities except for athletics.

> **Student government:**
> > **Girls: 27%**
> > **Boys: 19%**
>
> **Music/performing arts:**
> > **Girls: 46%**
> > **Boys: 35%**
>
> **Yearbook/newspaper:**
> > **Girls: 26%**
> > **Boys: 21%**
>
> **Academic clubs:**
> > **Girls: 36%**
> > **Boys: 28%**
>
> **Athletic teams:**
> > **Girls: 49%**
> > **Boys: 63%**

Conlin, 2003

Chapter 4

Pain, Anger, and Rage

Testosterone tends to be a misunderstood hormone. It does *not* cause aggression, according to Drs. Dan Kindlon and Michael Thompson (1999). While most boys experience a huge surge of testosterone in early adolescence, not all boys display aggression. Before age 10, boys and girls have roughly the same amounts of testosterone, yet the behavior of boys is quite different, even at 18 months. Boys tend to be more active, and their emotions are typically acted out rather than verbalized. Without the words, feelings that cause pain are often suppressed, leading to anger, and may at some point erupt into rage. The violence that has played out in America's schools in recent years is an example of this progressive emotional state in many boys.

Dr. William Pollack, author of *Real Boys* (1998) and *Real Boys' Voices* (2000), talks about the "boy code" that is ingrained in Western culture: BIG BOYS DON'T CRY! He says that big boys *do* cry and, if they don't, they'll cry bullets instead. Certainly every angry boy doesn't pick up a gun. The bullets, however, also can take the form of any of the following:

Alcoholism
Drug addiction
Workaholism
Sexual promiscuity
Inability to maintain personal relationships
Eating disorders
Obsessive spending of money
Obsessive hobbies
Obsession with movies, sports, television

Such behaviors and tendencies keep most males so busy and distracted they don't have to deal with their emotional pain. Being engrossed in one or more of these things helps keep the emotional pain at bay. The behavior is driven (largely subconsciously) by: "If I feed my obsession and stay focused on that, I don't have to deal with the emotional me." As noted in the previous chapter, some males mask this in what is called an "attitude." This is the "armor" protecting the male from pain. The armor presents the tough exterior and communicates to the world that he can't be hurt. Furthermore, no one can see who he really is. It becomes the impenetrable mask.

A report by **ABC-TV News** focused on the release of dopamine in the brain from ages 15 to 19. Research done by Yale University psychiatrist Andrew Chambers suggests that dopamine triggers a "go" signal in the brain (Dye, 2003). Drugs, sex, and video games stimulate the brain, making it want more drugs, sex, and video games. They're also finding that there are many factors that trigger the release of dopamine, including food, stress, and trauma.

So why do some young people experiment with drugs, sex, and videos, while others do not? Scientists believe that a common denominator is motivation. Young people who are motivated to make something of their lives — those who have hope and are future-oriented — are less likely to experiment with things that might divert them from their goal. Chambers found that boys and girls who experiment with drugs, alcohol, and tobacco during adolescence have a higher rate of addictive behaviors as adults than those who do not. A genetic predisposition or a social situation — coupled with an inclination toward impulsiveness or reckless choices with little regard for the consequences — makes a teenager more vulnerable to addiction.

For boys the risks are proportionately greater. Given the hardwiring of the male brain, most boys already have a predisposition to take risks. They are driven to be competitive and to win; they are more physically active and have a real need to move. How many girls have you seen spinning and jumping around on a skateboard, a dirt bike, or motorbike — or conquering the bronco or bull in a rodeo?

For boys in poverty, the risks increase even more. Time in poverty is about the present, not the future. If there is no future, where is the motivation? Poverty also has its own code for boys. In poverty the role of the male is to be a fighter and a lover. Fulfilling this dual role begins at a very early age for many boys in poverty where the male is expected to fight, be tough, stay strong, and maintain a stiff upper lip. The results are:

- Higher stress levels.
- High motivation to get physically strong.
- Increased sexual activity at younger ages.
- Experimentation with drugs, tobacco, and alcohol.
- Motivation to belong to a group/gang.
- Frequent use of non-verbals to communicate.

The triggers for a boy's pain can be numerous and varied. The deep-seated causes of the pain, however, are more closely connected to the resources that a boy is missing. If a boy gets into trouble in school he may not like it, but the emotional fallout from the incident is more closely associated with the resources that are lacking within the boy himself and/or his home environment.

In *A Framework for Understanding Poverty* (2013), Dr. Ruby Payne defines poverty as "the extent to which an individual does without resources" (p. 7). Resources are essential to survival. The fewer resources one has within the family, the more trapped one becomes by circumstances. The resources Payne identifies are:

- Financial.
- Emotional.
- Mental.
- Spiritual.
- Physical.
- Support systems.
- Relationships/role models.
- Knowledge of hidden rules.

For boys to survive emotionally without resorting to rage, they must be able to access their resources. When the resources are lacking in the home environment, boys must be able to access them elsewhere if they are to survive their emotional pain. Because boys are inclined to retreat to their "emotional rooms," their pain often leads to anger and rage. The degree to which the following resources are *lacking* contributes to the intensity of a boy's emotional pain. Boys tend to feel that their only resources are the ones *they* have; accessing what the family has to offer is not always perceived as a viable option. Real men stand on their own two feet.

- **Financial resources:** For a boy to participate with his peer group requires money. To be able to date a girl requires financial resources — the car, the clothes, the movie tickets, etc. To be involved in certain extracurricular activities requires that the boy be able to pay the necessary fees and

 other related expenses. To be with the "in crowd" can at times be very expensive. Members of that crowd might decide to spend Spring Break in Cancún, or they may pressure him to bring along a six-pack for a little fun.

  Many boys lack the financial resources necessary to fit in with their perceived in crowd. To want to belong to a certain group, only to be allowed periodically to peer in the window, is painful. That pain, if unattended, can lead to anger and rage.

- **Emotional resources:** Emotional resources are necessary because they are internal resources and show themselves through stamina, perseverance, and choices. When the boy comes home from school with a note from the teacher seeking a conference to discuss the student's behavior, how does the parent respond? Emotional resources are lacking if the parent curses or yells at the boy — or hits him. If alcoholism or drug addiction is present in the home, this resource is lacking. Parents who don't have the emotional stamina to deal with problems — and who don't regard problems as an integral part of life — lack this resource. Students unable to control their anger when confronted by a teacher or fellow student lack this resource. Physical fights may result when emotional resources are lacking. Students who act on their anger before stopping and thinking lack this resource. Boys who can't deal with their breakup with a girlfriend and resort to drinking, yelling at the girl, or acting out in a destructive manner lack this resource.

- **Mental resources:** Some students and parents lack mental resources. Being able to read and write to deal with daily life, which includes having a facility with language, are crucial coping skills. Some parents are unable to read the notes their children bring home from school. (Another complicating factor related to mental resources, but in a different category: Many parents in immigrant families haven't yet learned English.) Students who are unable to read, for whatever reason, may mask their frustration by acting out. One dyslexic adult described himself as a bully when he was in school. He explained, "You make people respect you in one way so they won't ridicule you in another way."

- **Physical resources:** Physical health and mobility are important for students who must cope with adversity. Some students, especially those from poverty, have increased incidents of diabetes and obesity. Experiencing shame because of one's size compounds problems for many boys. Poverty also deprives many boys of appropriate medical care. The lack of medical care can result in physical disparities that are very important to adolescent boys' self-image, such as access to a dentist or a dermatologist. As noted earlier, to be the "fatso" or a perceived weakling can be the kiss of death with peers.

- **Support systems:** It's important to have friends and backup resources to access in times of need. For many boys, the aloneness that comes from the lack of support systems enhances their pain and anger. For the boy whose father isn't available, where does he turn when he has questions about shaving, how to tie a tie, the father-son athletic event, or how to deal with a bully? Some boys feel very alone in such times because they lack external support systems. An adolescent boy's support system often becomes other

boys who are in as much pain as he.

◆ **Relationships/role models:** Many boys lack positive relationships and role models. Even in intact families some boys are very alone because their father is emotionally detached. Boys need frequent access to male adults who are appropriate, who are nurturing, and who don't engage in self-destructive behavior. Where does a boy learn that it's OK for him to be different from the crowd — and still be an "all right" guy? In poverty, boys may be exposed to many men whom Mom brings home. They aren't always the most appropriate role models. Boys in poverty frequently don't have access to Little League baseball, soccer teams, Boy Scouts, swimming lessons, chess club, karate lessons, and other organized sports and activities where strong male role models are giving leadership.

◆ **Knowledge of the "Boy Code":** The linchpin of the boy code is that boys don't cry. Males who don't understand the boy code become victims of it. They're teased and taunted for not being a "real man," a "tough guy." Boys who embrace the boy code, "BIG BOYS DON'T CRY," bury their feelings inside and often feel alone and misunderstood. They have no place to go with their emotions, and they have few words to describe what they're feeling. When fathers also "buy in" to this idea, boys are driven even farther away because they don't have appropriate role models to help them deal with their internal struggle. Boys who understand the implications of the boy code weigh their options when making decisions that might subject them to teasing or even ridicule. They know when they're breaking the boy code and are more likely to be able to handle the repercussions. For example, the boy who wants to be a cheerleader when the school has never had a male cheerleader knows he'll be teased. Parents who are aware of this code also can help their son examine his choices and let him know they'll be in his corner regardless of what he decides.

Boys who lack a number of these resources, as well as the words to articulate the corresponding feelings, tend to act on those feelings in socially unacceptable ways. For them to cope with their feelings, they must have a vocabulary to deal with them. Educators must incorporate the teaching of a feeling vocabulary into the curriculum. Without a feeling vocabulary, boys are left without labels for what they feel. The result is "acting out" behaviors, most of which are unacceptable in a school setting. Learning about the connotations of words that describe a range of emotions is essential. Words are needed for both negative and positive feelings. A list of words that shows this emotional range follows.

- **Feeling powerful:** aware, proud, respected, appreciated, important, empowered, successful, worthwhile, valuable, confident, good, renewed.

- **Feeling peaceful:** nurtured, trusting, loving, tranquil, thoughtful, contented, thankful, secure, serene, lovable, pensive, contemplative, relaxed.

- **Feeling joyful:** excited, terrific, energetic, cheerful, hopeful, daring, exhilarated, thrilled, fired up, stimulated, amused, playful, optimistic.

- **Feeling scared:** afraid, frightened, confused, rejected, helpless, submissive, insecure, anxious, bewildered, discouraged, insignificant, inadequate, embarrassed, overwhelmed, alone, abandoned, desperate, trapped.

- **Feeling mad:** hurt, hostile, angry, selfish, hateful, skeptical, critical, distant, sarcastic, frustrated, jealous, annoyed, irritated, upset, distraught, put-down, unimportant, minimized.

- **Feeling sad:** tired, bored, lonely, depressed, out of sorts, ashamed, guilty, sleepy, apathetic, isolated, inferior, stupid, remorseful, hopeless, disillusioned, disappointed, weak, powerless.

Adapted from "The Feeling Wheel,"
developed by Dr. Gloria Wilcox,
St. Petersburg, Florida

Use the above list as a springboard to developing a Feeling-Word Thesaurus for the classroom. When boys cannot come up with words about how a character might feel — or regarding how they feel about something — ask them to get the Feeling-Word Thesaurus and try to find a word that comes close, and we'll start talking from there. The Feeling-Word Thesaurus also can be very useful in the principal's office or the counselor's office.

The brain is not a thinking machine; it is a feeling machine that thinks. Everything that goes into the brain first enters at a sensory level. Words are used to label the feelings to give them meaning. If words are not present to label feelings, then a person literally becomes a prisoner of his or her own emotions. Words are absolutely essential for liberating the mind regarding emotions. Children who have experienced trauma (sexual abuse, physical abuse, seeing their mother battered, drive-by shootings, Hurricane Katrina victims, etc.) often bury their feelings. Later, these feelings may translate into post-traumatic stress syndrome (or disorder) and manifest themselves in acting-out behaviors, depression, alcoholism, or drug abuse as means of coping. In order to deal with these emotions, a third party, such as a psychologist or psychiatrist, is needed to help the person hook into the emotion, label it, process it, and cope with it. Many angry boys have virtually no words to label their emotions, and they become trapped in those emotions, subsequently manifesting their anger in destructive ways.

Dr. Howard Gardner in ***Frames of Mind*** (1993) explains the importance of feelings as follows: "The less a person understands his own feelings, the more he will fall prey to them. The less a person understands the feelings, the responses, and the behavior of others, the more likely he will interact inappropriately with them and therefore fail to secure his proper place in the world" (p. 254).

> When an individual shows empathy toward another person, that person perceives the individual as an ally.

Chapter 5

One Boy's Journey

> "Without boundaries,
> it's very difficult to articulate
> a personal code of ethics
> or have a sense of integrity."
>
> —The Emotional Abyss
> p. 27

The percentage of women between the ages of 25 to 34 with at least a college education, plus advanced degrees, outnumbers males in most industrialized countries, including:

Australia

Canada

Finland

France

Japan

Spain

United States

Conlin, 2003

Chapter 5

One Boy's Journey

About Eric …

- White male, age 34, from an upper-middle-class family.

- He is a gifted adult.

- Both parents are high school graduates. His mother has some college hours, and his father has a doctorate.

- He has a sister seven years younger.

- Both parents grew up in poverty. His mother's father was an alcoholic.

As are so many of today's children, I too am a child of divorce. While this certainly isn't unique in today's society, it was unique to me.

For the first nine years of my childhood, life seemed normal. I played soccer and baseball, and I loved to ride my bike. But when I was in 4th grade, my parents decided to separate. I had no voice in this decision. For that matter, I couldn't remember seeing my parents even argue. To me everything was fine; everything was normal. However, as time would soon tell, my life would forever be changed.

The relevance of this experience to me was discovered only recently as I was a 33-year-old adult coming out of a failed marriage, financial ruin, and a battle with alcohol addiction. I knew all these "flaws" were somehow connected, and I finally decided I had to find out how.

I'll be the first to admit … the choice to "fix" myself really wasn't much of a choice at all. Had it been left up to me, I would have certainly traveled down the same path for as long as possible. But things had gotten to the point that my behaviors weren't just affecting me anymore, they were affecting the ones I loved.

IN THE BEGINNING

Soon after my parents separated, I began to use food as a source of comfort in my life. At age 9 I had no way of articulating the emotions I was experiencing. At the time, I reached out to food for comfort. All my life, I was a normal-sized kid who looked and acted like so many kids we see today. But once my world came crashing down around me, I needed something to numb the pain. Before my 10th birthday I had become addicted to food. Eating was something to do. It kept me occupied and, yes, it seemed to help that weird feeling I always had in my stomach — a feeling I can now label as anxiety.

As the years passed, my weight increased. Each year, more and more weight. Food became a crutch. I needed it. Food was my friend, and I could get it anytime I needed it. But what began as a means of comfort evolved into a source of pain, as I was now an overweight adolescent with all the accompanying problems and stereotypes the "fat kid" must endure.

THE TEEN YEARS

All through school, I felt out of place. With my weight increasing, I was unable to wear all the cool clothes and never seemed to quite fit in. With food as my main source of comfort, my body became a physical reflection of my emotional state.

My first addiction (food) had now become a primary cause of pain, not relief. And, as I had dealt with the pain of my parents' separation years before, in my teens I sought out another external solution to an internal conflict. Just as I had chosen food in elementary school, in high school I chose alcohol.

School itself wasn't too bad for me. I made the Honor Roll and National Honor Society — and was even on the math team at one point. But I always felt I was in over my head. I just knew everyone would eventually see that I wasn't smart enough or good enough to be in the "in crowd." But I still needed to belong and to be accepted. I just wanted to be *normal.*

In 10th grade I had my first drink. It was great. I was funny. People liked me. I finally felt like I belonged. In hindsight, I now see that drinking was just an extension of what food provided as a 9-year-old. Alcohol could do for me what food never could. Alcohol actually numbed the pain. You see, I didn't truly realize the impact of my parents' separation. Therefore, I never looked for ways to work through the emotions and their accompanying self-destructive behavior patterns.

Having not really dealt with the emotions that began this cycle of events, I had developed a pattern of trying to solve internal conflict through external means. However, my methods of coping only led to their own unique additions of pain and suffering. The confused and scared 9-year-old soon became overweight, which, in turn, led to the teenager and young adult who became an alcoholic.

THE YOUNG ADULT

I followed this pattern for a number of years. I always knew I could — and should — do better, but it was all so difficult for me to achieve. I graduated from high school and went to college. But the freedom afforded an 18-year-old going away from home for the first time was simply too much to handle. I continued my practice of dealing with adversity through self-destructive means. I didn't know how to budget my time, study, or (for that matter) effectively take care of myself.

These feelings of uncertainty and insecurity, while on a more complex scale, were basically the same as when I was 9. Though I was now in college, the young adult was using the same techniques as the child. My drinking increased, and I started experimenting with drugs.

For a few years I did drugs regularly. But, as I would be thankful for later in life, I never could take drugs without alcohol. They just didn't do much for me. Now, in recovery circles, alcohol would be termed my drug of choice. It was a gateway drug. But just as food before it, once I reached a certain level, I needed more. Drugs simply became an extension of the alcohol.

Increasingly, I spent more time using alcohol and drugs. Most of my money went to numbing my pain. As my addictions worsened, I could no longer pay my bills. I was heading down a path of becoming so far in debt that my addictions eventually robbed me of nearly everything I had or cared about.

The majority of my 20s I continued on the same path … sometimes good, sometimes bad. I dropped out of college and had to find a job — one I eventually lost because of my first DUI (driving under the influence). I moved back in with my mom, stayed with friends and, yes, for a few days, even lived in my car.

A couple of years later I got a second DUI. By this time I didn't have any money. I couldn't afford a lawyer and had to sit in jail for a month. For the first time in my life, I was forced to think about my life as never before. I admitted to myself that I had a problem and accepted the fact that I had to quit drinking. And … I did.

For the next three and a half years, I was sober. I didn't go through a treatment program or attend Alcoholics Anonymous (AA). I simply stopped drinking. Of course, this in and of itself was a wonderful thing for me. During that time, I lost 60 pounds, started my own mobile DJ business, went back to college, and graduated with a BA in communications. And I got married; my best friend became my wife.

Not surprisingly, however, the positives didn't last. Although I had quit drinking, I hadn't learned the skills necessary for coping with life. So, without the information and support of AA or counseling, I began dealing with the complexities of married life in much the same way as I did when I was younger. What should have been the happiest time of my life was doomed from the start. I reverted to my old habits to numb the pain. I gained all of my weight back, plus 60 pounds more, and began drinking again.

Of course, this didn't solve anything, and it only added to the personal misery that was my life. But it didn't end here. Now that I had a good job and credit cards, I tried to buy myself into normalcy. I guess I figured that if my life was this screwed up, the least I could do was buy all the things I thought I needed for everyone else to think I was normal.

By again using external means to address internal issues, I now weighed 330 pounds, had become an alcoholic who ended up getting his third DUI, and was now in debt to the tune of $40,000! It was at this point that the woman I married, my all-time best friend, told me, "ENOUGH!"

On Memorial Day weekend of 2001, I moved out of our house and into a small one-bedroom apartment. It was over. After years of living through these vicious cycles, I had become an outcast in the town I had lived in for years. I had ruined friendships, relationships, and now a marriage. I was no longer able to hide from myself, because I was all I had left. In short, I hit "rock bottom."

A New Beginning

The first few months after my marriage broke up were the toughest, and it would be great to say that's when I started to get it together. However, the truth is, it took me a full six months before I started heading in the right direction.

The healing process started with counseling, followed by AA and, ultimately, my involvement in an outpatient program. It was through this effort that I was able to go back and get to the source of many of my behaviors. I finally realized that most of my struggles stemmed from a 9-year-old boy's inability to deal with his circumstances. With this knowledge, I became able to speak to my parents almost 25 years later to explain to them what I thought and how I felt about the entire situation.

You see, although I don't consider myself a victim or blame either of my parents, there was still a 9-year-old kid inside me who had to tell his parents how he felt. He just needed the vocabulary of a 33-year-old adult. I especially recall that my dad, the author of this book, and my mom took the time to listen with their heart to what I had to say. It was a healing time for all three of us.

While I cannot tell you things are perfect, I can tell you my life is much better. With every passing day, I gain more and more strength from the experiences I have endured. And, though there are still people who will have nothing to do with me because of the pain I caused, I have made amends as much as I know how.

I've now made a home for myself, made new friends and have been sober for two years. I've lost more than 110 pounds and just recently straightened out my financial situation. I go to church, take care of my body, attend regular AA meetings, and volunteer my time working at an Adult Literacy program.

But that's not quite where the story ends. While these moments of self-discovery and healing may seem overwhelming, realize that I did the majority of this work while I was searching for work. For more than 14 months I was unemployed, all the while living alone and trying to provide for myself. But this time I was equipped with tools and knowledge on how to better handle such a stressful time. During these months I experienced doubt, uncertainty, and even fear, but how I dealt with these emotions was diametrically opposed to the dead-end coping techniques I had used most of my life.

By keeping myself strong in mind, body, and spirit, I have persevered. When I felt the weight of my circumstances closing in, I focused on the progress I had made instead of looking at how far I yet had to go. I no longer turned to food or alcohol as a means of escape or comfort. Instead, I focused my energies on what I could do rather than waste my effort on things I couldn't do.

I stayed true to my diet. I changed, manipulated, and improved my workouts. Last (but certainly not least), I kept talking to those who were closest to me. I was determined to recognize the fact that things weren't exactly as I would wish them to be, but I trusted that I had done all I could to make my situation the best it could be for that moment in time.

I have now become the architect of my life. I've constructed my life with the stability of friends and activities that support a positive progression forward. Not only did these elements play a vital role during my 14 months out of work, they will continue to play a large part in my movement forward. I'm sure stresses and difficulties will forever be present in my life, but how I choose to deal with them will ultimately make the difference.

My friends and family serve as an invaluable source of motivation and encouragement. Without them, my journey would have been much more difficult and not nearly as rewarding.

But the greatest gift of all is the realization that I no longer need external "remedies" to correct internal strife. I now know that the power to heal and rise above adversity lies within. It is this underlying approach to life that will transcend any activity or relationship I have from here on.

And while there are no guarantees in life, one thing is certain: Somewhere inside, a 9-year-old boy smiles again.

Eric, 34

Chapter 6

Shame on You!

"Without empathy,
conscience can't develop."

—The Emotional Abyss
p. 27

"Gay and lesbian youth,
even those who aren't gay,
but are perceived as such,
face an unspeakable harassment
and abuse in schools ...
[T]he average high school student
hears 25 anti-gay slurs daily and ...
97 percent of high school students
regularly hear homophobic remarks."

"Bullies," 2009

Chapter 6

Shame on You!

Boys will do just about anything to keep from experiencing shame. In school shame often is triggered by teasing and name-calling. To be called a nerd, geek, girly, teacher's pet, mama's boy, crybaby, sissy, fag, gay, queer, fatso, four eyes, school boy, or any other derogatory term can be the kiss of death. As with shame, boys also will do almost anything to avoid being teased, even if it means compromising who and what they are.

In the field of psychology, guilt and shame were once considered synonymous terms. By about the mid-1980s, however, psychologists recognized that shame is a deeper emotion than guilt.

A simplistic way of thinking about the difference is that the emotion of guilt results when someone does something he/she realizes is wrong. The guilt can be rectified in one of two ways:

- By understanding that whatever happened is not one's fault.
- By apologizing and/or seeking forgiveness and thereby making amends.

An example of the latter: A child takes $5 from his mother's purse without her knowledge or permission. He feels guilt, knowing it was wrong or fearing he'll get caught (or both), confesses, and offers to repay the money and accept the consequences.

The emotion of shame is not as easily overcome. A boy participates with other guys in bullying another boy. After they torment the boy over a period of time, he commits suicide and leaves a note blaming the bullies. The boys experience shame for their behavior, but how do they deal with what they did now that the victim is gone? Shame runs deep; it is a more complex emotion than guilt. Boys — especially young boys — who suffer sexual abuse and physical abuse can feel great shame. They feel as if everyone knows. Other sources of shame can be:

- Where one lives.
- How one dresses.
- Where one's father and/or mother works.
- A parent in jail.
- Siblings or parents who are subjects of ridicule.
- Poor grammar, inability to speak English, accent, drawl.
- Not the "right" school supplies.
- Having been held back at school.
- Means of transportation.
- Inability to participate financially with the "in crowd."
- Acne, poor teeth, unkempt personal hygiene.
- Overweight/underweight.
- Poor at sports.
- Shunned by girls.

Because perceptions of masculinity in Western culture tend to be driven by strong, macho images, adolescent boys often experience insecurity, even shame, when they're discovering their sexual identity. Boys are pressured by their male peers to lose their virginity. For a boy in high school to verbalize to his friends a position of sexual abstinence increases the likelihood that he will be branded as gay. Having no one to talk with about these feelings and issues leaves a boy alone with his fears — and often his shame.

For African-American boys, Hispanic boys, and boys from poverty, these feelings are usually even more intense and difficult to deal with. Resting on top of gender expectations is a cultural overlay. This overlay for African-American boys, Hispanic boys, and boys from poverty often is considerably stronger than it is for most white boys and for middle- and upper-class boys of all races. These images are perpetuated both culturally and through the media. Getting good grades, for example, isn't in the macho paradigm. One of the biggest obstacles for these bright boys to overcome is dealing with their peer group labeling them a "school boy." To be a school boy is perceived as a rejection of both race and gender. Boys of color and those who excel academically are often accused of "acting white." This message from peers is all the more shocking if the inference is that only white boys have the capacity, or the right, to be intelligent and successful.

Indeed, there are models of excellence from all racial, ethnic, and cultural groups. Boys may wear cornrows, bandannas, or crew cuts. They may speak with an accent, a drawl, or another language. Being the best they can be must become the goal for all boys, especially for boys of color and boys from poverty.

VOICES FROM WITHIN

Inside one's head are three voices that control the tone of messages sent, as well as received: the parent voice, the child voice, and the adult voice. Intertwined are three basic components of communication: a message, a sender, and a receiver.

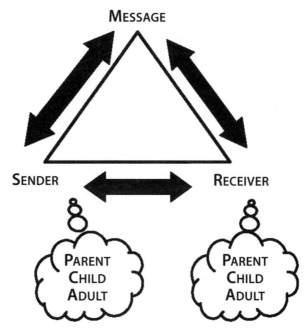

- The *parent* voice typically is filled with words of advice about what others should, could, or must do.
- The *child* voice is the whiner — the powerless victim.
- The *adult* voice asks clarifying questions and avoids judgmental statements.

For boys, two of these three voices often ignite problems in school. The teacher who has a strong parent voice tends to rob boys of their personal dignity and respect. Teachers who have a strong need to control use a parent voice. Boys seldom respond to the message per se; they respond instead to the voice and its tone.

PARENT (TELLING)	CHILD (WHINING)	ADULT (ASKING)
You shouldn't do that. It's wrong to … That's stupid, immature. You're good, bad, worthless, beautiful (any evaluative comment).	Quit picking on me! You don't love me! I hate you! Why me? It's your fault. You made me do it.	I need … What's your plan? What are your choices? If you did know, what would you say?

When a teacher uses the parent voice to demand compliance — "Sit down! Be quiet! Get to work! Stop talking!" — boys will respond in their own parent voice, either out loud or subverbally. Examples: ignores the teacher, mimics the teacher, sulks, or says, "This class sucks!" These are interpreted as a lack of respect for authority, non-compliant behavior, insubordination, lack of cooperation, or threats to a teacher. What the boy is trying to do is "save face" in front of his peers. Boys from poverty tend to perceive the teacher's oral demands as a challenge to their manhood.

Boys from poverty typically have two voices: a parent voice and a child voice. The parent voice is appropriate when safety is an issue and the adult in charge needs to deal with something dangerous or potentially dangerous ("Put those scissors down now!"). The parent voice does little, though, to change underlying attitudes that result in behavior. (The adult voice, on the other hand, has the potential to change behavior.) The child voice is whiny. The child sees himself or herself as a powerless victim. Some teachers also use a child voice to induce guilt as a means of trying to control group behavior ("You guys never listen to me; you don't show me any respect; look at all I've done for you, and this is the thanks I get; they don't pay me enough to put up with this"). It may work temporarily, but it won't last.

The adult voice seldom criticizes — or, if it does, is constructive. It seeks to understand the other person's point of view and attempts to guide that person through a process of clarifying what choices he/she may have. It validates the person's feelings, thoughts, and ideas. The parent voice largely invalidates those feelings, thoughts, and ideas. For boys this is crucial. The adult voice allows the boy to experience dignity and respect because it sets up a win/win situation. The parent voice is a win/lose position. For the boy who responds to the parent voice with a parent voice, it becomes a lose/lose situation.

Teacher: Parent Voice Student: Parent Voice LOSE/LOSE	Teacher: Parent Voice Student: Child Voice WIN/LOSE
Teacher: *"I'm not telling you again. Get to work."* Student: *"Yeah, yeah …"* Teacher: *"You better change your attitude, young man."* Student: *"There's nothing wrong with my attitude. Why don't you change yours?"* Teacher: *"That's it! Go to the office. I'm not putting up with you anymore."* Student: *"That's cool. I'm outa here!"*	Teacher: *"I'm not telling you again. Get to work."* Student: *"I don't understand what you want me to do."* Teacher: *"If you had been listening instead of talking, you would know what to do."* Student: *"You just don't like me."* Teacher: *"I don't like your attitude."* Student: *"You just don't want me in your class."*

Boys perceive female teachers with a strong parent voice as just one more "bitchy" mother. Male teachers who use a strong parent voice tend to be seen by boys as bullies.

Boys quickly lose respect for the teacher who uses a child voice. This is even truer for boys from poverty because weakness is scorned in poverty. The adult voice is important because it evokes dignity and respect for all parties. It's an affirmation of the person. The dignity and respect of both parties are preserved.

The thoughts, feelings, and ideas of the other person are taken seriously and validated.

Teacher: Child Voice Student: Parent Voice	Teacher: Adult Voice Student: Adult Voice
LOSE/WIN	**WIN/WIN**
Teacher: *"I have asked you three times to get to work. Please do as I ask."* Student: *"I don't feel like working."* Teacher: *"I've done everything I can to help you, and this is the thanks I get."* Student: *"Well, maybe you should try harder."* Teacher: *"You just don't appreciate anything anybody does for you."* Student: *"Well, maybe you have to actually do something before I can appreciate it."*	Teacher: *"You seem to be having trouble getting started on the assignment. How can I help?"* Student: *"I don't know."* Teacher (leans over student's desk): *"Tell me what you think you're supposed to do."* Student: *"I think we're supposed to outline the chapter."* Teacher: *"That's right. Review with me the steps we have learned about outlining."* Student: *"I'm not sure."* Teacher: *"That's OK. Let me see if I can help you clear up the confusion."*

ALL PEOPLE SEEK VALIDATION!

- ◆ Validation as a person whose feelings are real and true.
- ◆ Validation as a person whose ideas, thoughts, and feelings have merit.

When this does not occur, overt behaviors are used to get the attention of those from whom we seek validation.

Behaviors are symptoms; they are not causes. Schools typically react to symptoms with the parental voice. They punish the symptom rather than get at the cause. Certainly some symptoms have to be controlled; however, to punish symptoms and do nothing else is to almost guarantee that the behavior will return at a later date. To change the behavior, someone must get at the cause of the behavior. What is triggering the undesirable behavior? Sometimes it's the parent voice of the teacher. Sometimes it's the instructional activity that triggers feelings of inadequacy. The boy who lacks the necessary skills to do the activity may feel overwhelmed and powerless. This feeling ignites the powerless child within him. Without the words to articulate such feelings, he resorts to overt behaviors. One effective strategy to get boys into their adult voice is to use the following acronym.

TAKE THE **HEAT**

H = HEAR

+ "What I hear you saying is …" (listen for the non-verbals).

E = EMPATHIZE

+ "If I were in your situation, I probably also would be upset."
+ "You are obviously upset, and I understand why you are upset."

A = APOLOGIZE

+ "I'm sorry this happened to you."
+ "I can't take back what has been done, but perhaps I can …"

T = TAKE ACTION

+ "What I would like to offer you is …"
+ "Would it help if I … ?"
+ "What would you like for me to do to help you in this situation?"

Following the preceding steps takes less than a minute. It validates the feelings of the boy and gets him into his adult voice.

Let's take a specific case in point: A student who is upset with his grade accuses the teacher of being unfair. To help the boy get into his adult voice in this situation and take ownership in his feelings, the teacher might say something like the following:

- **Hear:** "What I hear you saying is that you think I was too harsh in the grading of your project."

- **Empathize:** "If I had been the student and you were the teacher, I might feel the same way."

- **Apologize:** "I'm sorry you feel that I have been unfair."

- **Take action:** "What can I do to help you understand how I came up with your grade?"

The above strategy also can be used with parents when they come to the school and use their parent voice or child voice. Emotionally healthy adults see problems, even conflict, as an integral part of life that can be solved and resolved. A parent with a strong child voice tends to be easily overwhelmed by problems. It isn't uncommon for parents from poverty to be "snowed under" by the demands of the school.

That phone call from the teacher can ignite the anger of a parent voice or the helplessness of a child voice — and the insecurity of both. When the child voice is present, the parent is powerless. For example: "I just don't know what I am going to do with him. He doesn't listen to me." This type of parent wants the school to just take care of the problem; make the pain/problem go away. These parents see problems as one more thing for them to solve, something they must fix when they may very well lack the know-how to fix it. When the school calls the parent who has a strong parent voice, he/she quickly gets ready to use "brute force" (mostly psychological, but physical on occasion) if necessary to resolve the problem. This can result in the parent being abusive to the student or verbally abusive to the school official on the phone or in person.

The adult who is rational (and uses the adult voice) resolves the issues and validates the feelings of others. The result is dignity and respect. It's a win/win situation. When the administrator summons the parents to the school because of a behavior problem with their son, school officials must be ready to deal with the emotional issues of the parents. The parents' feelings must be validated before the boy's problem can be dealt with.

Parent: Parent Voice School Official: Parent Voice	Parent: Child Voice School Official: Parent Voice
LOSE/LOSE transformed to **WIN/WIN**	**LOSE/LOSE** transformed to **WIN/WIN**
School official: *"Mrs. Jones, we are not going to put up with your son cursing at teachers."* Parent: *"Well, if Billy cussed at the teacher she probably had it coming."* School official: *"Regardless of what the teacher did, your son cannot do that."* Parent: *"Well, if you people would do what you're supposed to do, Billy wouldn't be a problem. It's not my job to run up here every day and do your job for you."* [School official shifts strategy to validate parent — HEAT.] School official: *"Mrs. Jones, what I hear you saying is that you don't think we really understand your son. If I were in your situation, I would probably feel the same way. I'm sorry we had to get you from work to deal with this. I know that is a hardship for you. What can I do to help you help your son? You obviously care very much about your son or you wouldn't be here."* Parent: *"I don't know what to do about him. Would you talk to him with me?"*	School official: *"Mrs. Jones, we are not going to put up with your son cursing at teachers."* Parent: *"I just don't know what to do with that boy."* School official: *"Obviously you haven't told him he can't curse at teachers."* Parent: *"I just don't know what to do. He's just like his daddy. I can't do my job and deal with him."* [School official shifts strategy to validate parent's feelings of inadequacy — HEAT.] School official: *"Mrs. Jones, what I hear you saying is that you aren't feeling very successful right now dealing with your son's behavior. As a parent myself, I know that isn't a very good feeling. I'm sorry we're having to put this on your shoulders right now. I know teenagers can be pretty overwhelming and that you care very much about your son. Otherwise you wouldn't be here. What can I do to help you and your son?"* Parent: *"I don't know."* School official: *"Would you share with me some things that you have been doing at home when your son doesn't do what he is asked to do?"*

The process inherent in "Take the HEAT" usually works because of the following:

1. **Hear:** It tells the person that you hear what he/she is saying and that you aren't just waiting your turn to talk *without listening.* This is achieved by really listening to the person, paraphrasing what he/she has said, and accurately portraying the non-verbals as well. The real message may not be the same message as the words spoken.

2. **Empathize:** To empathize is to let others know that you understand not just their actions but also their feelings. Empathy is essential if one is to feel validated as a person. When school officials skip this step in a parent conference, they'll have a difficult time getting to the real issues. Until the parents' emotional needs are met, the parents cannot deal with their son or daughter's emotional needs.

3. **Apologize:** This step is Part 2 of the validation process. (It isn't enough for me to know you understand, I also want to know that you wish I hadn't needed to go through this, experience, this conference, etc.) It lets the parent know you're sorry — in the sense of regret — that this situation has happened.

4. **Take action:** This is the step that summons the adult voice. When the person is asked, "What can I do to help you fix this situation?" you are putting the monkey on that person's back in a helpful way. They have to come up with the solution. Adults take responsibility. This step forces the parents to take some ownership in not only the problem but also in the solution.

If the parent is still in his/her child or parent voice after going through this 30- to 45-second sequence, begin the process again. Usually the second time through will do the trick. The key is not to allow the parent to put the monkey on *your* back. Parents are responsible for their own happiness, which means they also are responsible for helping find solutions for their own turmoil, issues, and conflicted feelings. This same process can be used between a parent and a child to help the child develop his/her adult voice.

A caring adult shows empathy for another person by using statements that validate the other person's feelings.

- "I'm so sorry that happened."
- "You must feel terrible."

- ◆ "That sounds like it really hurt."
- ◆ "I understand why you would be angry/sad/worried/upset."
- ◆ "You're showing a great deal of courage talking about it."
- ◆ "I know what you mean."
- ◆ "I'm really impressed with the manner in which you're handling this."
- ◆ "I regret you have been in this position."
- ◆ "I see why you feel uncomfortable in talking about this."
- ◆ "Tell me more."

For boys to develop empathy they must have adults around them who model empathy. Educators are in a position to do this on a daily basis.

Systemically, schools can put male students in positions that place them in no-win situations. When this type of thing occurs, boys are induced to assume the parent voice. The following analogy illustrates this dynamic.

Scenario #1: A man and a woman get married and have a child. Later they divorce. The father has visitation rights every other weekend. The mother tells her son to tell his father this weekend to buy him some new tennis shoes.

> **Mother:** "You tell your dad you need some new tennis shoes. That child support just isn't enough to buy everything you need."

That weekend, the son tells his dad what his mom said.

> **Son:** "Dad, Mom said you need to buy me some new tennis shoes. She said you don't give her enough money to take care of everything I need."

> **Dad:** "Well, you can just tell that mother of yours that I send her plenty of money, and if she wouldn't waste it on stuff for herself, she could buy you those shoes. I send her that money for you, not for her! I'm not buying you those shoes, and you can tell her I said so. A million dollars wouldn't be enough for that woman."

Son returns home.

> **Mom:** "Did you get those tennis shoes you needed?"
> **Son:** "No. Dad said you waste my money. He said you should be spending the money on me instead of yourself."

When a child is put in the middle of two angry adults with strong parent voices, the child is likely to get frustrated, especially if he/she is young. But as children grow, they often learn to be manipulative, and they are put in a position of power. They can translate Dad's and Mom's statements in whatever ways they choose.

Scenario #2: The teacher has asked Johnny three times this week to bring poster board and glue to school for a project that is due on Friday. On Wednesday she reminds him again.

> **Teacher:** "Johnny I have asked you three times this week to have your mom take you to the store to get some poster board and glue for your project that is due this Friday. Now when you go home tonight, you ask your mom to take you to the store so you can get your poster board and glue. We're going to finish up our projects in class tomorrow, and you must have your stuff."

Johnny goes home. When his mother comes in the door, he delivers the teacher's message.

> **Johnny:** "Mom, my teacher said for you to take me to the store and get some poster board and glue so I can do my project."

> **Mom:** "Well, you can just tell your teacher that I am not made of money. She makes a lot more than I do, and if you need it she should just buy it. Besides, there's enough kids sniffing glue as it is. I'm not about to buy you any glue."

Johnny returns to school without the supplies.

> **Teacher:** "Johnny, where are your poster board and glue?"

> **Johnny:** "I forgot."

Johnny cannot tell the teacher everything his mother said. In time Johnny will learn to be manipulative because both the teacher and the parent are putting him in the power seat. If he doesn't like his teacher, the translated message the student delivers might not be so pleasant.

Teachers and school officials need to talk with parents and take the student out of the middle. Healthy families don't use children to deliver messages to other adults. Healthy systems don't put children in the middle, creating a lose/lose situation for the student.

SPARE THE ROD, IMPROVE THE RELATIONSHIP

The manner in which boys are disciplined often adds to the shame they're experiencing at school. Despite how it may sometimes appear, boys don't come to school with the intention of getting into trouble. Most overt behaviors surface when a boy lacks the skills necessary to deal with his emotions. When school officials react to the behaviors in a parent voice and use punitive measures, they may resolve their frustration, but they rarely change the behavior of the student. When a school official is using his/her parent voice, a boy usually reacts to the emotional tone, not the words contained in the message. Vocal tones reflecting criticism and even rejection are heard. The advice contained in the message goes unheard.

Boys raised in homes that use authoritative measures may, on the surface, respond to the authoritative school official by appearing remorseful and stop the behavior. The pain, however, is still there. If unattended, the pain grows to anger. Boys from poverty who haven't learned to control their impulses may take the punishment, but the behavior seldom changes. Boys from poverty have a different frame of reference for punishment. In poverty, punishment is about forgiveness, not necessarily change; it's the penance for the crime. In *A Framework for Understanding Poverty*, Ruby Payne explains that "love tends to be unconditional in generational poverty, and because the time frame is the present, the notion that discipline should be instructive/redemptive and change behavior isn't part of the culture" (2013, p. 107).

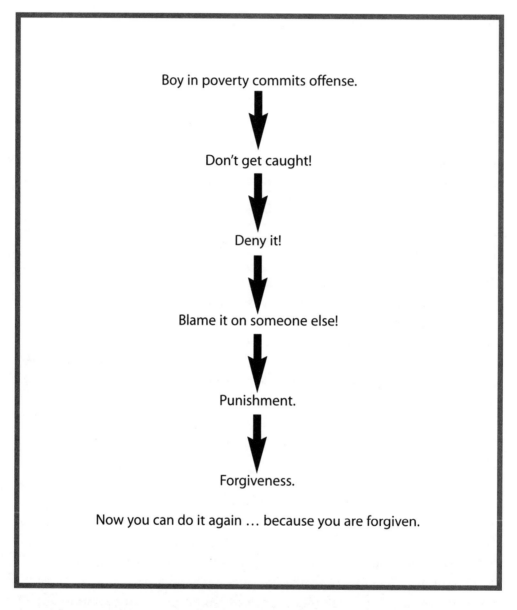

Boy in poverty commits offense.

Don't get caught!

Deny it!

Blame it on someone else!

Punishment.

Forgiveness.

Now you can do it again … because you are forgiven.

For boys to learn self-control, words must be used to explore the feelings behind the behavior. Using words to punish a boy is usually ineffective. Boys become focused on the emotions being conveyed, not on the message being delivered. Lecturing a boy, especially in front of his peers, is demeaning and reinforces his feeling that school isn't a friendly place and that school officials don't like him. The boy must know he is cared for, even when his behavior is unacceptable.

A significant way that caring is communicated is when the school official gives the student an opportunity to process alone. Boys need to have a shame-free time to process their emotions. They have a need to "retreat" in order to better understand their own feelings. At school this retreat setting can be achieved by asking older boys to write about the incident, while younger boys can be asked to draw pictures of what happened. Giving boys a "time out" area also can create a shame-free space. Boys need both time and space to come up with words that will articulate their feelings once they're ready to talk. Orally criticizing a boy generally compounds the problem. Criticism tends to cause one of two reactions.

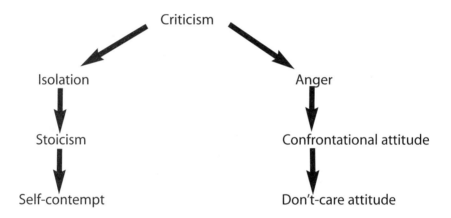

The reaction by most boys to criticism is a mask, a more or less blank visage or visual affect. What's running through the boy's mind are the following kinds of thoughts:

- "If I show fear, I'm not a real boy."
- "If I say I'm sorry, I'm a wimp."
- "I have to take it like a man! I'll show 'em I don't care."

School officials would do well to listen to both the verbal and the non-verbal messages that boys communicate. Behind the mask is usually a boy who is either frightened or very angry — sometimes both. School officials have a choice: They can stoke the fire that fuels the anger, or they can help the boy extinguish the burning embers. To put out those embers, someone must help the boy find his voice and express in words his feelings to a non-judgmental adult. As painful as it may be to realize, school officials and teachers who consistently use the parent voice actually model bullying behavior for students. To be sure, school systems are judgmental by design. Students receive judgments about their academic performance on a regular, almost daily, basis. (And there are non-academic ways that students feel the sting of school judgments as well: not making a sports team, not getting a coveted part in a play or a musical, losing an election, etc.) To work at something and then receive a poor grade is never easy to accept. When students consistently fail at their academic tasks, they become even more sensitive to the manner in which the adults in the school treat them. Most students who excel academically aren't frequent offenders of school rules.

Students who don't experience academic success, however, are reminded often that they are somehow less than others for whom it all seems to come so easy. When teachers add fuel to the fire by drawing attention to their inappropriate behaviors, the feelings associated with failure and inadequacy are further inflamed. In time the embers are restoked, and the fire is well on its way to becoming a roaring inferno.

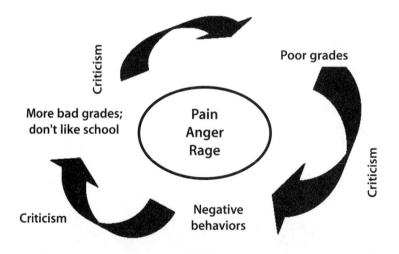

Chapter 7

Mixed Signals

"He will bully those who are
different and vulnerable.
His weapons are
words, fists, and guns."

—The Emotional Abyss
p. 27

"Many boys are diagnosed with
attention-deficit disorder,
or its companion,
attention-deficit hyperactivity disorder."
Boys consume 80%
of the world's supply of Ritalin.
That is an increase of 500%
over the last 10 years.

Conlin, 2003

Chapter 7

Mixed Signals

ust as oil and water don't mix, honesty among boys doesn't always lead to respect. Rather, the result often is shame. Boys who experience ridicule — or feel ridiculed — frequently experience shame, which ends up in emotional scarring. The bully, those who are bullied, and those who observe from the sidelines … all may experience some degree of shame.

A study of 1,200 Hispanic 9th-graders from urban and rural districts in Texas (Willoughby, 2002, p. 47) found that, overwhelmingly, the bullies were males, older, larger, and a higher grade level than the ones being bullied. Of the teachers and administrators included in the survey, 62.49% felt that teachers sometimes bullied students, and 74.99% felt students sometimes bullied teachers. Bullying is a learned behavior and continues when adults look the other way, refuse to recognize it, or dismiss it as "boys will be boys."

Young gay boys often bury their true feelings, resulting in a shameful secret from family, friends, and sometimes themselves. Gifted boys, "geeks," "nerds," or dancers/artists who also happen to be gay, black, Hispanic, Native American and/or poor experience an even greater emotional crisis. The majority of boys lack the verbal facility to navigate such turbulent waters. Couple that with the fact that there tend to be precious few socially acceptable forums for expressing such differences, and one can readily see why many boys are in crisis.

Any one of these scenarios may result in teasing by male peers. Being judged, criticized, and even humiliated by family and/or peers results in shame. Persistent invalidation of thoughts, feelings, and ideas reinforces feelings of inadequacy. Those who are invalidated become vulnerable targets for bullying because they probably will be the prey that won't fight back or "squeal." Isolation and feelings of aloneness become these boys' ever-present companions.

In *The Bully, the Bullied, and the Bystander* (2003), Barbara Coloroso identifies some of bullies' common traits. Bullies …

- ◆ Dominate other people.
- ◆ Lack empathy.
- ◆ Concern themselves only with their wants, desires, and pleasures.
- ◆ View their victims as their "prey."
- ◆ Refuse to accept responsibility for their actions.
- ◆ Lack the ability to foresee consequences of their behavior.
- ◆ Crave attention.

The bully often masks his own feelings of inadequacy behind an arrogance that says, "I am better than you." It is a mentality that clearly says, "It isn't enough that I succeed; you must fail."

Bullies pounce on just about anything — race, gender, religion, mental abilities, physical attributes, or sexual orientation — as an excuse to bully others (see list below). Coloroso makes a distinction between teasing and taunting. She describes teasing as playfulness between two people in which both find humor. The motives are innocent and not intended to destroy. Taunting, however, is destructive. It is one-sided and is intended to harm another person or group. The laughter is not shared; it is targeted toward someone. Taunting induces fear and loathing in another person or a group.

Bullies can target a boy for almost anything, including:

- ◆ Being new to the school.
- ◆ Being younger than classmates.
- ◆ Being a follower.
- ◆ Being anxious or excited about something.
- ◆ Lacking self-confidence.
- ◆ Having an annoying habit.

- ◆ Being shy, reserved.
- ◆ Being poor or rich.
- ◆ Expressing emotions easily.
- ◆ Being gifted, bright, talented.
- ◆ Wearing braces, glasses.
- ◆ Talking with an accent.
- ◆ Having acne or other skin condition.
- ◆ Having a physical or mental disability.
- ◆ Having an unusual first or last name.
- ◆ Being perceived as having feminine behaviors, characteristics, or mannerisms.
- ◆ Being fat, thin, tall, or short.
- ◆ Dressing differently.
- ◆ Voicing a different point of view.

It doesn't take much to become the prey when a predator is on the prowl.

Where does the bully learn to be a bully? The first and most influential teacher is the family; the second, according to the research, is teachers at school. Coloroso describes three basic types of parents and teachers:

- ◆ Brick-wall.
- ◆ Jellyfish.
- ◆ Backbone.

Brick-wall and the jellyfish parents and teachers help create bullies. More on backbone parents and teachers in a minute.

Brick-wall families are extremely authoritarian and rigid. They are very concerned with rules and order and have a well-defined power structure. Children are to obey at all costs. Children's feelings are often ignored, ridiculed, negated, criticized, made fun of. Children are humiliated (including in front of others), physically and psychologically punished, threatened, and shown love and affection only when they comply with directives. A strong parent voice rules in the brick-wall family. Brick-wall parents manipulate their children with emotions.

Appropriate, nurturing relationships and role models are in short supply or simply don't exist. Brick-wall parents lack an adult voice and an emotional vocabulary. They tell their children **what** they are to do; such parents say little about **why** or **how**.

In the jellyfish family there is a lack of structure. Coloroso places jellyfish families in two categories.

Type 1: This jellyfish family provides little or no structure for children. These are parents who are permissive and allow children to go to bed when they wish, eat when they want, with few day-to-day routines. Family life is chaotic at best, out of control at worst. Jellyfish parents tend to be enmeshed (sometimes called negative fusion) in their children's lives, rescuing them at every turn. They manipulate their children largely through bribes and threats. Discipline is lax, and limits are seldom set.

Type 2: These jellyfish parents are physically or psychologically absent in relation to their children. Such parents are focused almost exclusively on themselves. Sometimes drug, alcohol, or mental disorders are present. They also can be so involved in their careers that they have almost no time to nurture their children. The kids in this type of jellyfish family are left with hopelessness and despair. The children learn that they must manipulate and lie to people to get their basic needs met. Because they feel unloved and abandoned, they trust very few people.

Jellyfish parents lack emotional resources. They grew up without appropriate relationships and role models and very limited support systems. Their own parents may have been brick-wall parents, and they know the pain of fear, as well as the fear of pain. They want very much for this not to happen to their children.

The third family type Coloroso describes is the backbone family. These parents don't have a power structure. They are more democratic and are non-violent. They negotiate. They live and model respect. Children in backbone families learn that they can disagree, yet their viewpoints will be listened to. Members of a backbone family learn how to love themselves and one another, as well as to have empathy for others. They are compassionate toward those who suffer and work to help them. The family is a peaceful structure that is consistent, firm, and fair. Discipline is handled with authority that informs the child what he/she has done wrong and why it's wrong. The child is given ownership in the problem and is offered ways to resolve the problem. Dignity and respect are present.

For children to become self-governing, three things must be present: choices, consequences, and parameters. Backbone parents provide all three of these. Jellyfish parents allow many choices with few or no consequences, and parameters are practically non-existent. Brick-wall parents permit virtually no choices, with plenty of consequences if a rule is broken, and parameters are everywhere; minefields abound in this child's life. Beyond the family, children learn bullying behaviors from teachers, including administrative personnel and athletic coaches.

Just as there are three types of families/parents, we find that teachers/administrators also fall into these same basic categories. Brick-wall teachers have strong parent voices and enter the classroom demanding respect. They lay down the rules and are ready to punish students at the first infraction. It's a power statement. It's almost inevitable that students who enter these classrooms with their own strong parent voice will clash with the teacher. These students are bullied by a teacher, and they learn how to bully from the teacher. Sarcasm is frequently the humor of choice.

In fact, many boys who are *physical* bullies with few words listen and learn at the feet of such sarcastic adults, whose oral putdowns of people, in effect, expand the younger bullies'"horizons." Most students fear the wrath or derision of the teacher, and the classroom is an oppressive environment where learning is all but snuffed out, a candle flame flickering in the wind. Brick-wall teachers see themselves as the one responsible for demanding respect for authority, the last line of defense in an increasingly disrespectful and chaotic world.

Jellyfish teachers are the permissive ones. To get students to do their work, they bribe and coerce them — or try to be their "buddy." These teachers attempt to get students to cooperate by rewarding them with videos, candy, free time, and anything they think might work. Their classrooms tend to be chaotic, and students are disrespectful to the teacher and their fellow classmates. These teachers do various things to try to get the students to like them, which may include trying to be "cool," talking in casual register, wearing the latest clothing styles, and sharing jokes with the students.

Another (somewhat less common) variety of teacher is an intriguing hybrid of the brick-wall and jellyfish "species." These individuals remain aloof from the students, teaching with little regard for their learning. They may take the stance that it's their job to teach and the students' job to get it.

Not much real learning happens in the classroom of the jellyfish teacher. Students learn to be manipulative. They try to talk the teacher out of giving the test, assigning the homework, counting the bad grade — and some will lie to get what they want. All too often the teacher succumbs to the manipulation.

The backbone teacher is one who is fair and firm. Students hear an adult voice in the backbone teacher, and all students are treated with respect and dignity. Students are encouraged — and have a right — to challenge and ask questions. Backbone teachers model appropriate questioning. Students know the expectations are based on them being successful. These teachers celebrate students' successes, and they're available to help the unsuccessful student. Students are never ridiculed or put down in front of others. If there is an infraction, the teacher handles it with the student one-on-one using an adult voice.

The classrooms of backbone teachers aren't based on control. Their classrooms are structured in a manner that increases the probability that students will make right choices. Backbone teachers are honest and accept their challenges in working with students seriously, professionally, and lovingly. Students want to be in their room because there they regularly receive validation as a person.

Students encounter their personal and school families on a daily basis. As a result, they're sometimes forced to survive in very different environments, adding to a confused student's already confusing world. Some are fortunate to get teachers who have the emotional resources that offset those that are lacking in the home. Some teachers develop healthy relationships with students in spite of the absence of these models in the home. In short, students from brick-wall and jellyfish families need backbone teachers.

The following charts reflect some of the parallel and conflicting key attributes of these three types of role models that appear in both the home and the school.

HOME AND SCHOOL ROLE MODELS

BRICK-WALL

HOME	SCHOOL
◆ Uses parent voice.	◆ Uses parent voice.
◆ Lacks emotional resources.	◆ Uses emotions to manipulate.
◆ Has great difficulty forming relationships.	◆ Remains distant from students.
◆ Uses physical force.	◆ Is unconcerned with students' feelings.
◆ Lacks feeling vocabulary.	◆ Focuses on content, classroom rules.
◆ Curses to express anger.	◆ Demands respect, whether earned or not.
◆ Doesn't access support system; feels that he/she doesn't need help.	◆ Accords student few rights, virtually no voice.
◆ Expects blind obedience.	◆ Feels that he/she doesn't need help from other teachers or administrators.
◆ Accords child few rights, virtually no voice.	◆ Threatens students.
◆ Gives affection only after compliance.	◆ Is highly competitive; promotes winning and losing in the classroom.
◆ Provides the what, not the how or why ("You do it because I said so, that's why").	◆ Uses sarcasm, even humiliation, as means of controlling students in classroom.
◆ Often uses threats, ultimatums.	◆ Blames parents, society, administrative policies for student problems.
◆ Uses humiliation, putdowns as means of extracting obedience from child.	◆ Almost never makes exceptions to his/her rules for anyone.

JELLYFISH

HOME	SCHOOL
◆ Uses child voice.	◆ Uses child voice.
◆ Punishes and rewards children inconsistently.	◆ Enforces school rules inconsistently.
◆ Uses threats and bribes.	◆ Shows favoritism.
◆ Is coercive.	◆ Responds on emotional level.
◆ Allows emotions to rule actions.	◆ Sometimes uses assignments, tests to punish/reward students.
◆ Defends child's behavior to others.	◆ Feels overwhelmed by student behavior.
◆ Loves child conditionally — if child pleases parent.	◆ Feels underpaid, describes administrators as being of no help.
◆ Sees self as alone with almost no support system.	◆ Acts impulsively.
◆ Seems overwhelmed with responsibilities.	◆ Manipulates students.
◆ Expresses emotions to get sympathy, cooperation from child.	◆ Uses external rewards to motivate students.
◆ Acts impulsively.	◆ Doesn't accept responsibility for student performance.
◆ Manipulates and can be manipulated.	◆ May express sympathy for students, not empathy.
◆ Sees self as victim.	
◆ Feels alone in facing life's problems.	
◆ Sees behavior as "phase child will outgrow."	

BACKBONE

HOME	SCHOOL
◆ Uses adult voice.	◆ Uses adult voice.
◆ Communicates love, acceptance through daily actions, words.	◆ Communicates deep concern for students' ideas, thoughts.
◆ Invites child to voice opinions; teaches how to do so appropriately.	◆ Conducts class meetings; establishes and practices democracy in classroom.
◆ Encourages child to compromise and build relationships.	◆ Uses respectful language; sets rules that are simple, consistent, fair.
◆ States rules simply, clearly.	◆ Validates students through words, actions.
◆ Facilitates problem solving by child.	
◆ Encourages child to develop plans to correct wrongs.	◆ Uses humor appropriately; avoids sarcasm, put-downs.
◆ Offers smiles, hugs, humor freely.	◆ Feels confident enough in self to express own emotions to students.
◆ Expresses feelings, thoughts, ideas in reciprocal environment.	◆ Creates classroom conducive to risk taking, critical thinking; challenges thoughts, ideas appropriately.
◆ Teaches child the what, the why, the how; expresses confidence child can figure it out.	◆ Fosters non-competitive environment.
◆ Trusts, listens, expresses emotions in safe environment.	◆ Doesn't use bribes or threats.
	◆ Feels supported by colleagues.
◆ Doesn't bribe, threaten.	◆ Focuses on self-improvement.
◆ Views problems as integral part of life, opportunities to learn.	◆ Sees classroom problems as routine part of teaching/learning process.

Chapter 8

Family Lessons

"He will remain
disconnected emotionally
from his wife and children, and
his relationships will disintegrate
or simply go unfulfilled.
The void remains."

—The Emotional Abyss
p. 27

Boy TV is a new audience that
advertisers are seeking
"… because they believe it to be
a largely untapped market
of emerging consumers.
Technically, the networks want
18- to 34-year-old men.
Off the record,
they'd be thrilled to get the
12- to 34-year-old male audience.

"To lure them in,
TV offers up
women in bikinis wrestling
in beer commercials.
It's why NBC ponied up
$10 million an episode
for a 10th season of 'Friends.'"

—"Guy TV," *Zest*
Houston Chronicle
July 6, 2003

Chapter 8

Family Lessons

Jason, a freshman in high school, has just received his first report card and is not looking forward to handing it to his mom or showing it to his dad when he visits him on Friday. Jason has gone from being a solid A and B student in middle school to barely getting by with all D's this marking period. When he gets home from school, he locks himself in his bedroom where he has access to his own cable-ready TV, Xbox console, and computer with Internet connection. He turns on the Xbox and picks up where he ended his online play at 2 a.m. His game of choice is "Call of Duty."

His mother begs him to come out of the room for dinner, and when he does, he spends most of his time at the dinner table with his smartphone. Mom asks him how things are going at school, and he responds with his usual answer: "Fine." She continues to ask questions until he finally blurts out, "Just leave me alone. Why are you always interrogating me?" He storms off to his room and continues his online game, finally falling asleep at 3 a.m. He reluctantly leaves his report card next to his mom's purse as he heads for school at 7:30 a.m.

Is this just an example of an adolescent boy going through puberty, or is there more to the story? Why do boys stay up all night to play video games, and what are the repercussions?

In a national survey of U.S. adolescent males ages 15–19 titled "Masculinity Ideology: Its Impact on Adolescent Males' Heterosexual Relationships" (1993), researchers Pleck, Sonenstein, Ku, and Burbridge found that boys who adhere to a masculinity ideology were more likely to:

- ◆ Drink beer.
- ◆ Smoke pot.

- Get suspended from school.
- Engage in unprotected sex.
- "Trick" or force someone into having sex.

There was high correlation among all groups who participated in the study: black, white, rich, poor, urban, and suburban. Four key questions were used in the survey to determine adolescents' views of masculinity ideology. They were asked if they believed in the following:

1. It is essential for a guy to get respect from others.
2. A guy will lose respect if he talks about his problems.
3. A young man should be physically tough even if he's not big.
4. A husband should not have to do housework.

What are the sources of this mythology? The home is probably where it begins. The role of fathers in the home and the relationship that exists between fathers and sons is key in helping boys shape their personal definitions of manhood. A positive adult male role model may be a substitute for this vital lesson in defining manhood if the biological father is not available.

The U.S. Census Bureau's report "America's Families and Living Arrangements: 2012" determined that of all households with children, more than 12 million were being raised by single mothers and more than 2.4 million by single fathers.

Some highlights of the report include:

- Sixty-six percent of households in 2012 were family households, down from 81% in 1970.
- Between 1970 and 2012, the share of households that were married couples with children under 18 halved, from 40% to 20%.
- The proportion of one-person households increased by 10 percentage points between 1970 and 2012, from 17% to 27%.
- Between 1970 and 2012, the average number of people per household declined from 3.1 to 2.6.
- Black children (55%) and Hispanic children (31%) were more likely to live with one parent than non-Hispanic white children (21%) or Asian children (13%).

The findings from the census report have profound implications for boys who do not have a father in the household, as described by Dr. William Pollack (1998).

Pollack reports several studies that underscore the significance of the father/son relationship.

- In a survey of 7,000 men, sociological researcher Shere Hite found that almost none of the males surveyed were close to their fathers.
- A study of 71 clients by Massachusetts psychologist Jack Sternback found that 25% had a physically absent father, 40% had a father who was psychologically or emotionally absent, and 15% had a father whom their sons found frightening or dangerous.
- In a study of 80 adolescent boys (Case Western Reserve, D'Angelo), it was found that fathers who had the poorest self-control, who lost their temper, and who acted out in impulsive ways had sons who demonstrated significant difficulties in most areas of their lives.

For boys from poverty who live in an emotional, concrete, sensory-based world with limited facility with language — and a frequently absent father — impulsivity is commonplace, coupled with the following effects:

- Poor grades in school.
- Poor or nonexistent conflict-resolution skills.
- Difficulty in getting along with peers.
- Problems with drugs and alcohol.
- Ineptitude at handling intimate relationships.
- Tendency to become sexually promiscuous.

Between 1970 and 1994 the percentage of black children living in single-parent families nearly doubled. By 1994, 60% of black children lived in one-parent homes (Pollack, 1998). The documented effects on children of fathers being absent in the home include:

- Diminished self-esteem.
- Depression.
- Delinquency.
- Violence.
- Crime.
- Gang membership.
- Academic failure.
- Difficulties with emotional commitments.

Fathers who are actively involved with their sons from infancy have boys who are less aggressive, less overtly competitive, and better able to express feelings of vulnerability and sadness. These boys are generally more empathetic. The more time fathers stayed close to their sons, the better the boys did in high school, college, and in the workplace (Pollack, 1998).

THE CHANGING FAMILY STRUCTURE AND FUNCTION

Boys belong to a family. The family structure is defined as the configuration or number of people within the relationship. Family function is defined as the extent to which a child is cared for and nurtured. Both structure and function are changing, and this has a potentially powerful effect on boys. Traditionally the nuclear family has consisted of two parents, along with brothers and sisters. Boys' extended family comprised grandparents, neighbors, godparents, and friends. Surrounding these were community entities that also were part of a boy's life. These consisted largely of school and church. Over the last 50 years the media have been added to a boy's community.

For our purposes, in the next three chapters (8, 9, and 10), the media will be defined as any form of communication that may influence decision making, including but not limited to the following: television, movies, pictures, music, print material, apps, video games, social media sites, and the Internet in general. The following diagram illustrates the hierarchy of the family as it existed for much of the second half of the 20th century.

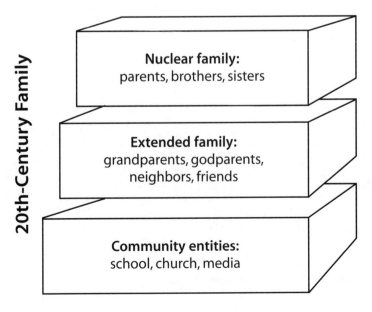

20th-Century Family

Nuclear family:
parents, brothers, sisters

Extended family:
grandparents, godparents,
neighbors, friends

Community entities:
school, church, media

Over time the family structure has shifted. An increase in the divorce rate, couples opting not to marry, individuals choosing alternative lifestyles, and absentee biological fathers and mothers have contributed to this gradually accelerating shift in the family structure in the United States. Today the nuclear family may well consist of single parents, grandparents raising grandchildren, brothers, sisters, stepbrothers and sisters, half-brothers and sisters, same-sex parents, and relatives raising children.

These changes also have affected the configuration of the extended family. Many grandparents are still in the workforce, and they may live thousands of miles from their grandchildren. In some cases, the grandparents or other family relatives are the parents. Neighbors seldom play the role they did 50 years ago. Suburban America may know its neighbors, but close friendships with those neighbors rarely exist. Schools are now a member of the extended family. Schools feed many children twice a day, offer before- and after-school programs, provide backpack programs that allow children to bring food and personal hygiene supplies home over the weekend, host Boy Scouts and Girl Scouts meetings, and make concerted efforts to get grandparents to come to the schools and make a contribution to students. Schools have become the extended family for many children, especially for urban America. In short, schools provide the academic and social structure for large numbers of young people today.

In addition to school, active community entities are still churches and other religious organizations, but increasingly service clubs and organizations have entered the mix. The media, which used to be simply one collective community entity, have now "moved." Moved in. The media are now an integral part of the nuclear family. The 21st-century family has changed.

21st-Century Family

single parents, stepparents,
same-gender parents, grandparents,
brothers, sisters, stepchildren,
half-brothers/sisters, and
THE MEDIA

Michael Gurian, author of *A Fine Young Man* (1998), defines a family member as someone who is a regular part of our lives and the lives of our children. Today a major new member of that family is the media.

Today the media may include network, cable, satellite, and Internet television, DVD videos, streaming movies, video games, printed magazines, online magazines, Vine, YouTube, and social media sites such as Facebook, Instagram, Pinterest, Twitter, etc. The list of social media sites continues to grow, and the influence the sites have is profound. The technological advances of portable media devices allow you access to any and all of the media, anytime you want, 24 hours a day.

Young people become more familiar with some celebrities and athletes than they do with family members. Grandmother may be seen once a year; some TV personalities are visited daily. The stories told via the media have become an integral part of the process leading to self-identity. Self-identity has taken on a life of its own through the use of technology. Selfies have become the means to identify who you are, and then those images are posted online for the world to see with little or no concern about the impact it may have on future employment, relationships, or acceptance into schools or organizations. "Sexting" (sending nude pictures) has created problems for teenagers, as well as adults, from all walks of life.

Historically young people learn about who and what they are from stories. The stories have been passed down through time via the Koran, the Torah, and the Bible; Aesop's fables; the Brothers Grimm; tribal elders in the African, Asian, and Native American cultures; traveling minstrels; town criers; grandparents; and great-grandparents.

Today young people are learning the majority of their stories from television, movies, and social media. You can become instantly famous not by doing great deeds for humanity but by becoming an instant celebrity on a "reality TV" show. Jay Leno on "The Tonight Show" proved constantly in his segment "Jay Walking" that people of all ages can more easily identify and know more about TV and movie personalities than they do their own elected leaders or historical figures.

Technology allows one to create an avatar (a computer-generated image that represents an individual) that, in the individual's eyes, becomes invincible, superhuman, and needs no one to help it survive. How do I then experience or learn empathy or sympathy? Empathy is developed through real-world interactions, not through video games or by hiding behind anonymous posts in an online forum where you do not see the pain of the person you are insulting or bullying.

Machines have become the medium for most of the stories children hear, absorb, tell, and emulate. Drummed into young minds time and time again through the media are messages about one's identity; how to deal with a crisis; how to handle money (consumerism); instant gratification; gender roles; parental roles; and meanings of integrity, honesty, morality, and codes of conduct. A video image, Vine, picture, or selfie is frequently more powerful than a thousand words, especially if the only words you hear or see are on a media device instead of communicating face to face. The tactile sensation of flipping through the pages of a book is being replaced by the slide of a finger on a tablet or smartphone. Are we controlling technology, or is technology controlling us?

"Image making is storytelling, and storytelling is one of the key ways young human beings gain identity" (Gurian, 1998). The extent of this impact is reflected in his statistics:

◆ The average U.S. household has its television turned on 47 hours a week, though it isn't always being watched. The average number of minutes per week that parents spend in meaningful conversation with their children is 3.5. In other words, the TV potentially has the child's attention about 800 times more than that child's parents!

◆ Sixty-six percent of American households have a TV on while they're eating dinner.

◆ By the time a child is 18, he/she will have spent 22,000 hours watching television, double the time he/she will have spent in classroom instruction and more than any other activity except sleeping.

◆ An average boy in America spends five or more hours a week seeing television commercials. By the time he is 21, he will have seen 1 million commercials.

◆ For every child born in America, a television is made. In 1990 *Connoisseur* magazine reported that 250,000 children were born each day. That same number (250,000) of TV sets were made each day in 1990.

- By the age of 16, the average American kid will have seen 200,000 acts of violence on TV. One-sixth (33,000) will have been acts of murder.

- The numbers of stories on the nightly news that deal with crime, disaster, or war comprise 53.8% of the broadcast. The percentage of airtime given to public service announcements is .07% (less than one-tenth of 1%).

- Americans watch 250 billion hours of TV annually. The number of videos rented daily is 6 million, while the number of public library items checked out daily is 3 million.

Gurian, 1998, pp. 210–211

Pediatrics, the official journal of the American Academy of Pediatrics, released a report on February 18, 2013, titled "Childhood and Adolescent Television Viewing and Antisocial Behaviors in Early Adulthood." The findings conclude:

- Time spent watching television during preschool years has been found to predict antisocial behavior at ages 6–11 years, and viewing time in adolescence and early adulthood has been shown to be associated with subsequent aggression.

- Boys spent more time watching television than did girls.

- Men also scored higher on the Aggression personality scale and the Negative Emotionality superfactor but lower on Positive Emotionality.

- Young adults who had spent more time watching television during childhood and adolescence were more likely to manifest antisocial behaviors and personality than those who had watched less television.

- Children who spent more time watching television also had lower Positive Emotionality as adults.

- The associations between television viewing and subsequent antisocial behavior were similar for boys and girls, even though antisocial outcomes were less common in women. (Robertson, McAnally, & Hancox, 2013, p. 442)

They further conclude:

More time spent watching television in childhood and adolescence is associated with antisocial behavior in early adulthood. These associations were not explained by preexisting antisocial behavioral problems, lack of parental control, socioeconomic background, or IQ.

We believe that identifying ways to reduce children's and adolescents' television viewing should be considered a priority for public health. (Robertson, McAnally, & Hancox, 2013, p. 445)

Parents can and should control the amount of time their children spend watching television and should consider the ramifications of having a TV in their child's bedroom.

With the continuous development and use of computers, tablets, and smartphones, the traditional use of television and movies is changing. Most TV programs and movies can be viewed through a variety of devices. Viewers can now binge-view an entire season of a program's episodes anytime they choose. Original black-and-white movies and TV programs from the 1950s are digitally enhanced with the addition of color. The technological advances in the production of movies, animation, surround sound, and the visual capabilities of high definition TVs and monitors are giving viewers a completely new experience as they watch a movie, TV show, or play a video game. What is the overall impact on viewers who see graphic, slow motion details of violent images while watching TV, movies, or video games? What is the impact especially on developing children?

In a 2010 review, psychologist Craig A. Anderson and others concluded "the evidence strongly suggests that exposure to violent video games is a causal risk factor for increased aggressive behavior, aggressive cognition, and aggressive affect and for decreased empathy and prosocial behavior" (American Psychological Association, 2013, n.p.). In essence what Anderson believes is that continuous exposure to violent acts while playing video games or watching acts of violence could have an impact on how aggressively someone responds to a perceived threat or disagreement. Does this mean that if you play violent video games, you will automatically become violent? Of course not; however, there needs to be some form of conversation with caring and nurturing adults about the difference between video game violence and real violence. If adults tell children that playing violent video games or watching violent acts in TV and movies will cause them to become violent, they will lose credibility with the child. The child may even question the adult by asking if adults become violent after watching a violent show. Most boys don't see video game violence as real; to them it is just a game.

Christopher J. Ferguson does not agree with all of Anderson's findings. Ferguson "claims that much of the research into video game violence has failed to control for other variables such as mental health and family life, which may have impacted the results" (American Psychological Association, 2013, n.p.).

If a student comes from an environment where he witnesses real violence, could this be the main factor contributing to why he may be violent, or is it because of media exposure to violence, or both? The debate rages on, and more research is needed to provide a definitive cause and effect.

Playing video games may fill the void of learning how to be a man if there is no man to teach a boy how to become a man. If the boy views manhood as having to be tough, solving problems on your own, being in charge, winning at all costs, and showing no weakness or mercy, then he can accomplish that in the confines of his room on the computer and not worry about the repercussions of failing in the real world. If I lose in the game I am playing, I can always hit restart and start fresh.

How should parents deal with the gaming issue? First understand the games your boys are playing. Learn the gamer's lingo. Talk with your boys about the game; let them show you how it works.

While playing an action-oriented or violent video game, players' blood pressure goes up, and their breathing speeds up, as well as their heart rate. This is the same effect that playing sports has for some boys. Chemicals such as testosterone, cortisol, and dopamine are released while the playing intensifies and may lead to gamers giving up food or sleep to continue playing. This behavior may manifest the same characteristics as any addiction.

Rosalind Wiseman, in her book *Masterminds and Wingmen,* gives some very sound advice for parents on how to reduce the battles you may have with your children about playing video games:

- ◆ Video games are part of the social fabric of boy's lives; it is part of their bonding experience with other boys.
- ◆ The conversation about the violence displayed in video games is no different than the conversation about violence in other media formats. There must be a frank discussion about violence in all aspects. Express your beliefs and values.

◆ Gaming may help some boys become problem solvers, creative thinkers, and if they play online, they can develop relationships (Wiseman, 2014).

As a parent you can establish guidelines for play and be consistent in your enforcement of the guidelines, limit the time that they can play games, and keep the gaming device out of their bedrooms and in a public place. Have them use headphones to eliminate the concern about sound. As your children get older, revise your guidelines and remain vigilant in the consistency of enforcement.

When boys learn what it means to be a man through the media, the messages they receive become significant. What is this new family member communicating to our boys? The lessons are recorded in the brain and, in all too many cases, replayed overtly through action.

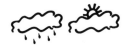

Chapter 9

The New
Family Member

"Without a conscience,
there is little sense
of right and wrong."

—The Emotional Abyss
p. 27

"Experts on child development speculate the 6-year-old boy who found a loaded, stolen .32-caliber pistol and used it to kill a 6-year-old classmate … was modeling the anger management techniques he saw at the movies, on television, through video games and at home."

"Model for Tragedy," 2000, p. 1D

Social media use in the USA:

+ 210 million active Facebook users (USA and Canada)

+ 74% of online adults use social networks

+ 52% of online adults use two or more social media sites

+ 356.9 million wireless subscribers

+ 90% of households use wireless service; 39% are wireless only

+ In a day the average American spends 159 minutes online via laptop/desktop and 134 minutes using a smartphone for non-voice applications

+ Hundreds of millions of hours of video are watched on YouTube per day

+ 300 hours of video are uploaded to YouTube every minute

"Average Daily," (2015); Duggan, Ellison, Lampe, Lenhart, and Madden, (2015);
"Number of Monthly," (2015); "Number of Subscribers," (2015);
"Social Networking," (2015); "Wireless Quick Facts," (2013); YouTube, 2015

Excessive television viewing during childhood and adolescence was associated with objective and subjective measures of antisocial behavior in adulthood. These associations were not explained by preexisting antisocial tendencies or other potential confounders. Excessive television appears to have long-term psychosocial consequences.

Robertson, McAnally, and Hancox, 2013

Chapter 9

The New Family Member

For centuries and across cultures, young boys have fantasized about doing battle with — and slaying — dragons and monsters. In their mortal combat with these creatures, the boys have jumped, flown, and leapt from walls and mountain peaks, attesting to their superhuman strength and indestructibility. Their roles had been defined through stories from their grandparents and tribal elders, along with written stories of knights in shining armor saving the world, not to mention the virtue of the beautiful maiden. Today all of those fantasies can be achieved through video games without having a conversation with anyone about the *what, why,* or *how* of the game.

Today the role of the male hasn't changed significantly. He is still a warrior, and he still must be indestructible, but the new setting for his conquests is the corporate world, a fantasy sports team, battling to victory in a video game, or bullying someone using social media sites. He also is perceived to be head of the household, even if his significant other makes more money or has a higher level of education. He is expected to protect his family from the perils of the world — and *always,* always be fearless.

Today it's largely the media that teach boys what it means to be a man. What messages are being communicated? Here are a half-dozen:

- If you have an enemy, it will probably be another male. (Competitiveness is hardwired in the brains of most boys.)

- Destroy your enemy. Male-on-male violence is pervasive. (You must win!)

- It's a cruel world, and people are out to cheat you and destroy you — and those you love. (With few words to articulate one's feelings, emotions rule.)

- If you cry, you had better cry alone. (Be brave. Never let 'em see you sweat — or let them see your weakness.)

- Females are sexual objects to be seduced, to be conquered. (Sex is the concrete and sensory-based definition of manhood.)

- In TV commercials (and infomercials) the male is to be physically fit with abs of steel. Females are attracted only to the good-looking jock. (The peacock must strut his stuff and show his colors.)

Messages communicated via the media are significant because while the adolescent brain processes everything it takes in, it is incapable of evaluating all the information. The adolescent brain is still developing. Adolescent boys need caring adults, especially male role models, who interact with them and solicit dialogue from them concerning the messages they are getting via film, TV, Internet, music, and commercials. The media have become the new teacher, and that teacher is the digital screen in the living room. (It may also be in the kitchen, bedroom, restaurant, the family's SUV, and anyplace that has Internet access and a power source to keep a handheld device powered up.)

For boys from poverty, the impact is even greater because of the concrete and sensory orientation of most impoverished people. Television seldom deals with complex and abstract ideas. TV focuses instead on personalities that are concrete and vivid. Commercials appeal to the senses — from sexual references and innuendo to physical attributes and appearances. Even news shows create entertainment out of news stories. Episodes of war are covered in a few seconds and feature live coverage on the battlefield with help from embedded correspondents. People who became president in the past may never have been elected in the present because they wouldn't "look the part." It's unlikely that today's president could walk with leg braces, be overweight, not be photogenic, or lack charisma.

Where is the caring parent/adult to help boys challenge what they see and hear? Needed is a parent/adult who asks:

- "**What** are they trying to sell you?"

- "**How** are they communicating that message?"

- "**Why** are they saying those things? Do they think we're so vulnerable, so stupid, or just so naïve that they can manipulate our thoughts, feelings, and ideas?"

The time from birth through adolescence is the most impressionable period for the human brain. During this period, the media make imprints on the mind about sex, violence, consumerism, and the ways (often degrading) that people interact with one another. This media bombardment makes fictional images seem real. This experience during a period of high cognitive development has a lasting effect on the male psyche.

For many boys, the media influence their view and now teach them what it means to be a man, and young boys get to rehearse their fantasies via video games and, in some cases, on the streets and in school. The media have become the new conduits by which a generation of young boys learns about its male identity. As the studies show, an alarming number of boys are not getting much help with identity issues from their fathers or from other adult males in their lives.

LIGHTS? CAMERA? ACTION!

How do media affect the brain? Studies show that male testosterone levels fluctuate according to the stimulation of media. Testosterone levels rise when males watch boxing and wrestling matches or view a hockey or football game. The brain becomes more agitated with the increased levels of testosterone. The testosterone acts like the paddles of a washing machine, stirring up the detergent that is resting calmly in the water. The agitation creates a chemical reaction in the washing machine, affecting everything inside. The stress hormone hydrocortisone rises in the brain.

Michael Gurian, in *A Fine Young Man* (1998), explains that even after a TV game is turned off, most males will appear to be more anxious and irritable. The bubbles in the washing machine don't immediately subside when the agitation stops. When males are bombarded with images on a consistent basis, the images become imprinted on the brain. Things that are highly sensory leave a lasting impression.

If as a child one awakened to the smell of bacon sizzling in the frying pan, as an adult that aroma may be recalled and trigger similar feelings. When Alfred Hitchcock's movie "Psycho" first came out, it sparked strong, even visceral, reactions; it made an imprint on the brain. One effect: being afraid to pull back a shower curtain for fear that "danger" would lunge forward, knife in hand.

Hitchcock's movies frequently left lasting impressions because they stimulated the reptilian part of the brain (survival-oriented portion) and the limbic system (emotive center of the brain). Remember your reaction to a flock of sparrows or starlings after watching Hitchcock's "The Birds"? Compare that reaction to the visually graphic and digitally enhanced sound of today's war films or horror films where there is little left to the imagination. Gore, blood, and sounds of death and destruction are now commonplace in movies, video games, cable TV, and network television programs.

Film has taken the world of print to a new level. With the printed word, the reader must think and create images. With film, the viewer processes but doesn't have to think. The viewer, therefore, doesn't necessarily have to evaluate what he/she views. Images from film can stay with us permanently. Without really understanding what one has seen, the mind is left with a new reality.

Gurian states that images create an imprint on the brain of both adults and adolescents. The difference is the degree to which the brain has to be bombarded in order to be brainwashed! With adults it takes much more than with adolescents. That process of imprinting is imagery. For boys with minimal words, those images are going to be sensory-driven. If a boy is exposed to sex, violence, materialism, and degrading social interactions during a period of high cognitive development, then he has a new and distorted sense of what reality is.

In action films, Gurian explains, images move faster than the brain can process them. The brain becomes overstimulated. These films create chemical reactions in the brain resulting in a type of addiction because the brain's self-protective mechanisms have been bypassed. The rapid pace of the action films produces fixated eye movements that in turn result in a visual consciousness, putting the mind into a state of relaxation that leaves it "off guard." It's the same sensation that a teacher observes in the classroom when a student is caught staring off into space, completely out of tune with what is happening around him. Gurian maintains that we have become a culture addicted to stimulants that move faster than our brains can handle. He states: "One of the prevailing contemporary theories as to why we in America suffer such high rates of depression, thought disorders (e.g., schizophrenia), and brain disorders (e.g., ADHD) is that our media/technology environment is too stimulating for our brains, whose process of neurotransmission still runs at a 'sane' pace, one that is more appropriate to the stimulation of a few hundred years ago. Media imagery runs at an 'insane' pace — that is to say, the stimulation of today is too much for the brain" (Gurian, 1998, p. 220).

During adolescence, reckless and impulsive behaviors are common. As noted earlier, this also is a time when the brain is undergoing tremendous growth and change. The prefrontal areas of the brain that enable us to do long-range planning, as well as consider the ultimate consequences of choices, is one of the last areas of the brain to fully develop.

Dr. Andrew Chambers, Yale University psychiatrist, and his associates found there are links between various stages of development that teens experience and the high rates of addiction that begin during the teen years. These researchers also discovered that "over 40% of adult alcoholics experience alcoholism-related symptoms between ages 15 and 19, and 80% of all cases of alcoholism begin before age 30. The median reported age of initiation of illicit drug use in adults with substance use disorders is 16 years, with 50% of cases beginning between ages 15 and 18 and rare initiation after age 20" (Dye, 2003).

Drugs, sex, and even video games cause brain cells to release excessive amounts of the neurotransmitter dopamine in the brain. The result is overstimulation of brain cells, which in turn disturbs normal thought processes and can lead to abnormal behavior. Dopamine acts as a type of green light in the brain, increasing the probability of poor choices among teens. Boys have a greater tendency to participate in risky behaviors during their teen years than girls. Boys are pressured by their peers to become sexually active sooner, to drink, and to experiment with drugs. Additionally boys between the ages of 8 and 15 are the biggest consumers of video games, which, along with action movies, reinforce these risky behaviors when they portray males as invincible, tough, beer-drinking, sexually promiscuous, macho guys.

How did we get to this point? Action films require little or no thinking. Comedy, on the other hand, requires translation, thinking. What makes something funny? Reading requires thinking. Without thinking, there is no meaning. Action films are emotion-driven, and it's a universal language. Filmmaking is driven by money, not just from the movie itself (theater, video, DVD, streaming) but from the T-shirt sales, action figures, posters, etc. In the '50s, movies didn't actually show a person being shot. The action was a smoking gun followed by one or more people falling down. One thing was certain: No blood was ever spilled.

During the '60s and '70s there was great social unrest in the United States. Movies increasingly began to reflect real-world violence. During the '70s African-American urban action movies (sometimes called "Blaxploitation" films) with shootouts weren't enough; audiences wanted more. So spectacular stunts were added. The boundaries that controlled language, sex, and violence have shifted over time, allowing more and more profanity, explicit sex, and gruesome violence.

"The French Connection" was one of the first modern films to include a chase scene. Clint Eastwood in "Dirty Harry" portrayed good guys taking on the social evils of the world. A long series of James Bond movies enhanced the macho image of suave crimefighter who repeatedly cheats death, then gets the girl — in bed. Technology and special effects enhanced the thrills in such movies as "The Towering Inferno" and "Poseidon Adventure." Eddie Murphy and Nick Nolte brought comedy to "48 Hours." High-concept storytelling was featured in "Robocop," "Top Gun," and "Flashdance." In the '80s sequels became popular with movies like "Rambo," "Rocky," and "Lethal Weapon." Arnold Schwarzenegger and Sylvester Stallone redefined the male physique. Chuck Norris and Bruce Lee in the '70s, Mel Gibson and Danny Glover in the late '80s and early '90s, then Bruce Willis in the '90s added to the male persona. They were the indestructible tough guys. Women also are becoming a major part of the action scene with movies like "Charlie's Angels," Demi Moore in "G.I. Jane," and Uma Thurman and Lucy Liu in "Kill Bill." What will be the new reality for a generation of young girls if this message gains in popularity?

With 21st-century technology, there's no limit to the creation of visual images to stimulate an audience. Today's action heroes do more than leap tall buildings in a single bound. They survive raging fires, rising floodwaters, twisting tornadoes, catastrophic car crashes, horrific explosions, and a steady stream of bullets — anything nature and the bad guys can throw their way. They have muscles of steel and are passionate lovers. They destroy villains (usually other men but sometimes alien creatures) with fists, guns, bombs, and knives, at times even devouring human flesh.

What was once accessible at the movies may now be rented or purchased for home viewing or streamed online shortly after the movie has left theaters. The 2014 hacking of Sony caused the corporation to make an unprecedented move to put the movie "The Interview" online rather than distribute it to movie theaters. This kind of on-demand access allows the same adult themes to be played over and over again at will. With available technology and Internet access, people can obtain any movie with ratings from G to X simply by clicking their remote control or streaming the movie to their TV or a mobile device.

Many families also have hundreds of channels from which to select to visually feed their minds. The line that used to separate movies from family television has become less and less defined. Sex, violence, degradation (often of women), profanity, and vulgarity are now part of prime-time television — or at least easily accessible. Cable and satellite TV have pornographic channels available 24/7, and unless parents have restricted the access, kids may watch these channels when unsupervised. Pornography is pervasive on the Internet, and adolescents and adults alike are becoming obsessed with the sites. The amount of time some viewers devote to watching these sites has created problems for themselves and their family members. Subjects that formerly were discussed discreetly are now openly described on daytime talk shows, soap operas, and the nightly news, including a United States president defining oral sex as not really sex ("I did not have sexual relations with that woman …").

If parents and educators aren't interacting with young people about these topics, and teens (and pre-teens) are processing the messages but not evaluating them, what conclusions will they draw? Across this country, more and more middle school students are engaging in oral sex, all the while declaring that they aren't really having sex. Ask a middle school teacher.

Because entertainment is a driving force for students in poverty, the impact of the media on boys from poverty is even more pervasive. The background of poverty sets up boys to be among the most vulnerable to the negative effects of the media. This vulnerability is a result of the following factors:

- Entertainment is one of the three driving forces in poverty (Payne, 2013). (*Life is tough; you need to have a little fun. Entertainment is a coping mechanism.*)

- Poverty is a concrete and sensory-based world. (*Action movies don't require thinking. They appeal to the senses.*)

- The focus of most action films, by definition, is on the action, not the plot. The physical strength of the characters is more important than the plot structure. (*Given the lack of formal register, much of the communication in poverty is non-verbal. And physical strength and toughness are greatly prized in poverty.*)

- Young people in poverty are left alone more than are middle-class American youths. (***There's seldom a caring adult asking what they're watching and how the TV show or movie is saying things and why. Without this intervention, or* mediation, *critical thinking seldom occurs.***)

- Impulsivity reigns in action films. A look often ends with confrontation. (***Impulsivity is more common in poverty because of its sensory orientation. "Stop and think" is not the typical mode of operation.***)

Reuven Feuerstein, an Israeli who worked with post-Holocaust Jewish young people, had studied under Jean Piaget, a Swiss psychologist. Piaget postulates that the brain processes information based on stimuli in the environment. Feuerstein contends that human intervention in this process could result in a different response. He labeled that process of intervention mediation. "Mediation is basically three things: identification of the stimulus, assignment of meaning, and identification of a strategy" (Payne, 2013, p. 121). The degree to which parents and other adults mediate reality for and with their children has enormous influence on the effects the media have on young people. Without adult intervention asking the what, the why, and the how, young people are left to process without the benefit of asking evaluative questions. This can result in a child or teen having a distorted view of reality. What is fact, and what is fiction? What is fantasy, and what is reality?

The popularity of "reality television" and shows sometimes described as "train-wreck TV" is one more indicator of a society that is fixated on stretching things to their outer limits. Adolescents are receiving messages daily about how to manipulate people and events in order to win ("Survivor" and its imitators). Messages about relationships are being communicated through TV's "Bachelor" and "Bachelorette" shows. The more popular shows rely on people's fascination with "cutthroat alliances, backstabbing, name-calling, hostile confrontations, exclusion and the art of exposure and attacking people's vulnerabilities" (Brown, 2002). The popularity of so-called "reality shows" that are designed to create drama and exploit relationship issues may be waning, but the negative behaviors they encourage and display are now entrenched parts of the entertainment industry.

The "reality" shows depict a form of bullying. Bullying isn't just a school problem anymore; it has become a national pastime. Parents can no longer say to their children, "This isn't real; people really don't do these things." On reality television real people are really doing these things. Students who watch these shows must be asked questions if they are to develop empathy, as well as a corresponding emotional vocabulary.

- *Why* do you think millions of people watch these shows?
- *What* do you think about how these people are treating each other?
- These are the same behaviors that get students in trouble at school, yet adults win thousands of dollars doing these same things. *What* do you think of that?
- *How* do you think people are reacting when they see these kinds of shows? *How* did you come to your conclusions as to what is good and bad about these kinds of shows?

It isn't the answers to these questions that are as important as the discussions that follow. Such questions produce critical thinkers. The questions force young people to stop and think. To do that, someone must be talking to the child.

Most of today's parents grew up having television as a family member. The large majority of them have never had a day without TV and access to it 24 hours a day, seven days a week. In many middle-class homes, both parents work outside the home. They come home tired, spend a little time with the family, and then it's time to go to bed and begin again. While dinner is being served, is everyone together? Or is each family member individually or collectively looking at their handheld device instead of having an interactive conversation? Do you have a "no media devices during dinner" policy in place? If the family goes out to a restaurant for dinner, they're likely to have access to a television there. Throughout America there are family restaurants with Dad, Mom, and the two kids eating dinner with all four sets of eyes watching up to a dozen TV sets that have no sound. No one is talking. The silence while watching the TV is broken only by the ringing of a cell phone.

The next time you go out to dinner, put away your portable devices and observe how many families, couples, or groups of friends are actually talking to each other instead of looking at their devices or watching a TV screen. Ask yourself: "What are the future implications for developing personal relationships or preserving culture if we do not know how to talk with each other?"

Who is developing the relationships among the family members? Television? Social media? Video games? Boys who are less verbal, who are reluctant to ask questions because guys don't seek help, are left with only the reinforcement of their peers — peers who are equally illiterate, both visually and emotionally — or they are left to their community of online gamers who are triumphant in their virtual world but may be suffering in silence about their limited real-world triumphs.

The Emerging Child-Adult Development

"He will cheat his employer by reporting expenses he did not incur, stealing the hammer he needs at home, calling in sick when he wants a day off, and blaming others for his mistakes. Everyone owes him."

—The Emotional Abyss
p. 27

"From age 2 to 17, youngsters in the U.S. spend a quarter to a third of their waking hours in front of a television screen. What's the harm? In a 17-year Columbia University study that tracked the viewing habits of 700 adolescents, 29% of those who had watched three or more hours of TV a day at age 14 had engaged in assaults or other aggressive behavior by age 22."

—*Parade*
September 15, 2002, p. 12

Chapter 10

The Emerging Child-Adult Development

Childhood, as a recognized developmental stage, is relatively new. Neil Postman, author of *The Disappearance of Childhood* (1994), points out that during the Middle Ages few distinctions were made between the roles of children and adults. The recognition of childhood as a separate stage in life, Postman argues, came about after the invention of the printing press, which gave rise to the mass production of books. Prior to the printing press, the clergy comprised Europe's educated, literate adults. With the advent of large numbers of books in print, an audience, a readership, became necessary. Out of that came the creation of schools. A population had to be developed who could read what was being put in print.

As schools evolved, rules of etiquette and decorum began to appear. Those who were teaching the young children noticed the youngsters doing certain things at certain ages. This gave rise to what educators called developmental stages in children. As noted above, educators also were responsible for creating heretofore unknown rules. Teachers and principals (originally the "principal teacher") were the ones who taught children to say "yes, sir" and "yes, ma'am." Fashion for children also began to evolve. How does an adult dress, and how does a child dress? There were rules for adults and rules for children, as well as roles for adults and roles for children. Lines of demarcation between adulthood and childhood had emerged.

Over the last 50 years, however, these lines have gradually faded. More and more children emulate adult behaviors — from the way they dress to the way they talk to the way they behave. School discipline is dominated by the enforcement of rules that often aren't supported even by the parents of the children. Why and how has this come about?

The significant difference between today and 60 years ago is the TV and the rest of the media. Children have learned adult behavior from the media. The media have influenced and sometimes replaced parents' traditional child-rearing norms that separated what were considered adult-only behaviors from child-only behaviors. Children of all ages have been exposed to a new set of behaviors that doesn't always distinguish between adult and child behaviors. Some children learn from the media what they used to learn from caring, nurturing adults. Few adult-only secrets or behaviors remain.

Postman maintains that if there are no adult secrets, there is no real childhood. Young people learn about the adult world from movies and commercials. Young children can hear on prime-time television the pros and cons of one sanitary napkin over another. What used to be left to the imagination of youngsters is now "out there," with most of the mystery removed. From daytime soap operas to prime-time sitcoms to TV commercials, sex sells products, and the youth market is worth billions of dollars. Elvis Presley and the Beatles pale by comparison with today's provocative dress, sensual lyrics, and dance moves. The boundaries have moved.

A popular commercial early in this century for a major soft drink manufacturer used entertainer Britney Spears and former senator and presidential candidate Bob Dole. While Spears promotes the product through a lively and sensual song, Dole is petting his dog and saying, "Down boy." What made it significant is that Dole also had done a commercial for Viagra and talked about erectile dysfunction (ED).

Children today are surrounded by adult themes. Passionate love scenes are part of the afternoon soap operas, as well as the evening sitcoms. Sexual references are an integral part of prime-time sitcoms. Relationships tend to be defined physically. Commercials use sexual imagery and innuendo to sell products that have nothing do with sex.

The significance of asking the **what,** the **why,** and the **how** is becoming increasingly important as children absorb the messages of commercials.

- When commercials have a mother and a daughter selling a product, and the question is which one is the mother and which one is the daughter, what message is being communicated to young people about one's looks?

- What is being communicated to young boys who watch men seeking out women based primarily on the women's sexiness? What price is being paid — by women *and* men — when the media portray women primarily as sex objects?

- How is the portrayal of women as sex objects complicated by commercialism? What messages are sent when advertisers use women's sex appeal to sell hamburgers, for instance, or cars?

- Why are increasing numbers of children committing adult crimes? Have we taught them how?

- Why do people want children punished for committing adult crimes? Have we as a society really addressed the real issue? What do you think is the real issue?

If no one is talking with children, especially during adolescence, what conclusions must they be drawing from what they see and hear?

Postman asks a piercing question: If there are no adult secrets, what is adulthood, and what is childhood? Is there a difference anymore? Schools reveal some common themes on a daily basis:

- Students show little respect for adults.

- Some parents wear T-shirts that communicate vulgarity or profanity. So what do you expect of the student?

- On TV sitcoms more and more language in the casual register is used as a form of humor. Students today imitate what they see and hear; schools, therefore, must insist upon and teach what talk is appropriate and inappropriate. No one seems to be teaching them that in the home.

- Parents defend a student's choice to use vulgarity and profanity and to wear provocative attire that is represented on TV as the fashion of the day.

- Parents curse at their children when disciplining them.

- School boards want zero-tolerance policies, thinking they will be a deterrent to violence and drugs at school.

Drugs have become the modern way to control behavior. The Centers for Disease Control and Prevention estimates that 6.4 million children ages 4 to 17 have been diagnosed with ADHD at some point, and about two-thirds of those currently diagnosed have been prescribed a drug like Ritalin or Adderall (Kant, 2013).

Perhaps the new family members (the media) are teaching our children things we really don't want them to learn, at least not yet. For boys, the messages are loud and clear.

- If you have an enemy, destroy him.
- You must be physically strong.
- If you are in a family setting, the woman has the brains.
- Women are attracted to you if you have sex appeal (good looks and a "hard body").
- As a male, you are expected to risk your physical safety in order to preserve your masculinity.
- You have greater sex appeal if you have money.
- Monetary status and physical attractiveness are more important than your intellectual abilities.
- Anger is to be expressed through aggressive action and aggressive language.

Television communicates visually; books communicate linguistically. The average length of an image on television is three to four seconds. The average length of an image on a TV commercial is two to three seconds. This requires that the viewer recognize patterns instantly. Reading requires analytical decoding; TV merely requires perception. These perceptions rely on concrete and sensory images. Television doesn't require knowledge of the alphabet, grammar or spelling lessons, logic, special vocabulary, or prior training. A study by Dr. Daniel Anderson, a psychology professor at the University of Massachusetts, found that children begin watching TV systematically at the age of 3 years and soon can replicate tunes, songs, and phrases heard on television (Postman, 1994, p. 79).

In impoverished households this information is particularly significant. In poverty, entertainment is important; the TV is almost always on. Television and the media appeal to the concrete and sensory composition of poverty. For boys from poverty, the aggression they see or hear via the media reinforces their impulsivity. The media make all information available, and through the Internet, access is almost instantaneous. Boys from poverty in single-parent homes often are viewed as the "man of the house." When the media make few distinctions between adults and children, and when the environment draws no such distinctions, children will talk to adults as if they are their equal. What has traditionally been perceived as good manners — showing respect for one's elders and others — has eroded.

Manners always were important because they call for self-restraint, and they created a social hierarchy. Manners are a social means of controlling impulsivity. Literacy creates an intellectual order. Literacy, the ability to stop and think about what one has read, is an academic means of controlling impulsivity. Thinking is essential to becoming a rational, productive adult in the workplace, the home, and the community.

Much of the media's output is driven by profit. As such, the media will continue to do whatever sells. Students, especially boys, must be taught to think about the messages they are watching. If no one asks the what, the why, and the how, boys will replicate what they see and hear because it will be their reality. Just as Prohibition didn't stop people from drinking, censorship will not keep people from producing commercials and films that sell. The solution is to produce skeptical and savvy consumers who question what they see and hear. To do that, one must stop and think.

Chapter 11

Symptoms vs. Causes: Six Case Studies

"He will vandalize
and abuse his surroundings;
the rules don't apply
to him ..."

—The Emotional Abyss
p. 27

"It stands to (his) reason
that if he doesn't put himself —
his feelings, his ego, his desires —
on the line,
then he can't get hurt."

McGraw, 2003

Chapter 11

Symptons vs. Causes:
Six Case Studies

Teaching and learning are interactive processes that frequently spark difficulties for both students and teachers. This is especially true for males who are less verbal. Unsatisfactory academic or disciplinary performance in school is often the result of missing resources. What resources are missing in the following *true* scenarios? In analyzing the causes, please be free to refer back to chapters 4, 6, and 7.

SCENARIO #1: JOSÉ

BACKGROUND

José: 11th grade, history of struggling in school.

Parents: divorced, father does construction work, mother is teacher's aide, José lives with his father.

English teacher: age 26, single, four years of teaching experience, female.

José is in the 11th grade. José's school history reflects four expulsions for fighting, beginning in the 7th grade. He was assigned to the district's alternative education placement program on two separate occasions. Since the 6th grade his academic performance has consistently bordered on failure; José's parents have appealed the disciplinary decisions of every principal, beginning in elementary school. His parents divorced when José was in the 9th grade, and José chose to live with his dad. His mother said she couldn't handle him and agreed to pay child support until José completed high school.

José's mother is a teacher's aide in a different school district, and his father does construction work. Both parents usually come to the school for the principal/parent conference when José gets in trouble.

RECENT INCIDENTS

1. In English class José is asked to read a part in a play the class is studying. His teacher notices that José is busy working on something at this desk and not paying attention. She asks him to read aloud. José refuses. The teacher approaches his desk and notices that he's drawing a caricature of her. The teacher says, "José, I guess you think that's funny. I don't deserve this! I'll take it." José refuses to give the picture to the teacher. The teacher tells him again to give it to her and asks that he open his book and read the assigned part. José remarks, "It's a stupid play. I don't want to read."

   "Well, if you aren't going to read and participate with the rest of the class, you can't stay in here. You can go to the office." She writes out a discipline referral and tells José to go to the office. He is charged with disrespect toward a teacher, not participating in class, and insubordination. Instead of going to the office, José leaves school. The discovery is made at the end of the day when the teacher asks the assistant principal about José's punishment.

2. The state in which José attends school has very stringent attendance laws. Students cannot miss more than 10 days a year without meeting very specific excused-absence criteria. Students who miss more than 10 days can't receive credit for course work, regardless of the class average. School officials prosecute students who exceed the absentee rate. A local judge has been very supportive of the state law and often fines parents if their child has habitual absences. He has on occasion required parents to miss work and attend classes with their child. José has missed 15 days between September 1 and November 1. School officials have reported his case to the local judge.

CURRENT STATUS

José's father requests a meeting with a top Central Office official. The father brings José to the conference.

Father: "I don't know what to do with him. I don't want to be responsible for him anymore. I can't pay the judge's fine, and José won't do anything I say. I asked his mother to take him, and she said she wouldn't be responsible for him. I even offered to pay her $200 a month if she would take him, and she said no. I know he can't drop out of school until the end of this school year because he just turned 17. He won't do anything. He is just going to get in more trouble, and I can't afford it. Is there a way he can be declared an adult so I don't have to be responsible?"

José sits quietly, looking down, making no eye contact with anyone.

School official: "José, what do you see as your options?"
José: "I don't know."

What are the symptoms?
What are the possible causes?
What are some possible solutions?

What resources do you think are present in the family, in the teacher, and in the student? Write **yes** if the resource is present, a **no** if it's missing, and a question mark (**?**) if you aren't sure.

RESOURCE	FAMILY	TEACHER	STUDENT
Financial			
Emotional			
Mental			
Physical			
Support systems			
Relationships/role models			
Knowledge of boy code			

What is the parenting style of José's parents?

       ___ Brick-wall   ___ Jellyfish   ___ Backbone

What is the teaching style of José's English teacher?

       ___ Brick-wall   ___ Jellyfish   ___ Backbone

Which voice does each of the following use?

José: ___Parent   ___Child   ___Adult

Father: ___Parent   ___Child   ___Adult

Teacher: ___Parent   ___Child   ___Adult

What are the symptoms and causes in the current situation?

What would you recommend to try to get José on a more productive path?

SCENARIO #2: MATTHEW

BACKGROUND

Matthew: age 7; 2nd grade; oldest of three children; has younger brother, age 4, and half-brother, age 6 months.

Mother: divorced, second marriage, two boys by first marriage, stay-at-home mom, some college, married to her current husband for two years.

Stepfather: doctor, highly gifted, first marriage, has been married two years, age 38.

Biological dad: visits his son every other weekend, good relationship between father and son.

Teacher: divorced, 15 years of experience, mother of two girls, age 36.

Matthew's 2nd-grade teacher has had three parent conferences concerning Matthew's disruptiveness in class. She describes him as a bright little boy who has difficulty paying attention. The stepfather has attended all the parent/teacher conferences; Matthew's mother hasn't attended any of them. The stepfather is a former student at his stepson's school, and he's a prominent member of the community. He has a successful medical practice.

RECENT INCIDENT

Matthew is given a note to take home to his parents. The teacher reports that Matthew is always talking, even after being told not to talk without raising his hand. The teacher asks the parents to talk with Matthew because he is becoming disruptive in the classroom and preventing other students from learning.

While the stepfather is trying to talk with Matthew at home about his behavior at school, Matthew keeps playing with his favorite action-toy figure. His stepfather feels Matthew isn't listening or taking the conversation seriously. After twice asking Matthew to pay attention, the stepfather takes a pitcher of water off the kitchen table and pours it over Matthew's head and puts the action figure down the garbage disposal. He says he won't put up with him not listening to him or paying attention to his teacher. His mother doesn't interfere with the stepfather's actions and reprimands of Matthew.

CURRENT STATUS

Matthew also has been riding his bike with training wheels. The stepfather has told Matthew that he should be able to ride a bike without training wheels, that he was too big to be using training wheels. Matthew says he's afraid he will fall. His stepfather takes the training wheels off the bike and says he isn't going to put them back on. Matthew is no longer trying to ride his bike because he's afraid of falling over. Matthew's teacher has become frustrated that nothing seems to be improving his behavior and has suggested that the parents might want to have a pediatrician check him out.

What are the symptoms?
What are the possible causes?
What are some possible solutions?

What resources do you think are present in the family, for the teacher, and for the student? Write **yes** if the resource is present, a **no** if it's missing, and a question mark (**?**) if you aren't sure.

RESOURCE	FAMILY	TEACHER	STUDENT
Financial			
Emotional			
Mental			
Physical			
Support systems			
Relationships/role models			
Knowledge of boy code			

What is the parenting style of Matthew's stepfather?
___ Brick-wall ___ Jellyfish ___ Backbone

What is the parenting style of Matthew's mother?
___ Brick-wall ___ Jellyfish ___ Backbone

What is the teaching style of Matthew's teacher?
___ Brick-wall ___ Jellyfish ___ Backbone

Which voice does each of the following use?

Stepfather: ___Parent   ___Child   ___Adult

Mother: ___Parent   ___Child   ___Adult

Teacher: ___Parent   ___Child   ___Adult

What are the symptoms and causes in the current situation?

What would you recommend the teacher do to help Matthew?

What is your plan for Matthew, as well as for relating to the stepfather and the mother?

If the current family dynamic continues, what problems would you predict might occur within the next five years? What are implications of this for school behavior and learning?

SCENARIO #3: ADAM

BACKGROUND
Adam: age 12, 7th grade, new student to the school.
Mother: prostitute, doesn't know who Adam's father is, doesn't live with Adam
    on consistent basis, dropped out of high school in 10th grade, leaves Adam
    with her mother when she decides to "take off for a while"
Grandmother: lives on Social Security, loves her grandson, dropped out of
    school in 8th grade.

RECENT INCIDENT
While attending his new middle school, Adam meets Sam. Sam is his very first
friend. Sam and Adam hang out together all day. They have several of the same
classes, and they have the same lunch period, so they eat together each day.
They talk about girls and write the names of girls on their forearms.

Many of the middle school students have begun wearing tennis shoes that have
blinking lights. At a local discount store Adam and Sam each buy tennis shoes
with blinking lights that are alike. Both Adam and Sam have a history of being
loners, and both lack many of the social skills their classmates have. The majority
of the students at the school are from middle- and upper-middle-income families.
Other students begin taunting the two boys when they show up at school with
matching tennis shoes. They are called gay and fags. Sam soon decides he needs
to separate himself from Adam. The friendship is over.

Adam is devastated and becomes very angry. He verbally lashes out at his
classmates. Arguments continue one evening between Adam and his classmates when they go to an Internet chat room and exchange obnoxious, hateful
remarks. Late that evening, Adam posts a detailed threat on a Dark Angel
Website stating he and a group of assassin friends from his former school are
going to kill students at his new school the next day. He lists the first and last
names of the students.

Remembering what happened at Columbine High School in Colorado in 1999, a
student forwards the e-mail to scores of other students. Parents are at the police
station within the hour. Other parents call the media.

The next morning angry and upset parents are at the school demanding that something be done. Also the next morning, as soon as Adam (who knows nothing about the firestorm his e-mail had ignited) gets off the school bus, he is escorted to the principal's office where he explains that he didn't have any assassin friends and that he isn't really going to do anything. He is just tired of the other kids always giving him a hard time, and he wanted to scare them. He says, "I wanted to hurt them as much as they hurt me."

The principal explains to Adam that he is in serious trouble. "You can't just go around threatening people, Adam," she says. "That is a crime. You could go to jail. Even if you get out of this, I don't want someone in my school who threatens other students."

Before Adam is put in the police car to go to juvenile detention, the officer tells him to remove his shoes so he can be searched. Adam asks, "You won't take off my blinking lights, will you? My best friend Sam has shoes just like this."

Adam's grandmother is notified. She doesn't know what to do. She explains to the principal that she doesn't have any money for a lawyer and doesn't have a car to go see Adam. The grandmother doesn't know where Adam's mother is or when she will return. Adam doesn't seem to understand why he's in so much trouble.

CURRENT STATUS
After conducting their investigation, the police decide they don't have sufficient evidence to prosecute Adam. A number of the parents of other students are very upset by this and bombard the district attorney's office, demanding that something be done. They also demand that the principal expel Adam from school.

The principal explains that the incident occurred off the school campus and she can't punish a student for something he did outside of school. She tells them it's a police matter, not a school matter. The parents threaten to take their children out of the school if Adam is allowed to return to the school.

What are the symptoms?
What are the possible causes?
What are some possible solutions?

What resources do you think are present in the family and in the student? Write **yes** if the resource is present, a **no** if it's missing, and a question mark (**?**) if you aren't sure.

RESOURCE	FAMILY	STUDENT
Financial		
Emotional		
Mental		
Physical		
Support systems		
Relationships/role models		
Knowledge of boy code		

What is the parenting style of Adam's grandmother?
    ___ Brick-wall   ___ Jellyfish   ___ Backbone

What is the parenting style of Adam's mother?
    ___ Brick-wall   ___ Jellyfish   ___ Backbone

What is the parenting style of the other students' parents?
    ___ Brick-wall   ___ Jellyfish   ___ Backbone

Which voice does each of the following use?

Grandparent: ___Parent   ___Child   ___Adult

Principal: ___Parent   ___Child   ___Adult

What are the symptoms and causes in the current situation?

What would you recommend that school officials do to help Adam and his grandmother?

What do you think the school should do with the complaining parents and the students involved in the taunting of Adam?

SCENARIO #4: RICKY

BACKGROUND

Ricky: age 10; 4th grade; very overweight; lives with his mother, stepfather, and two half brothers; well-liked by his teachers who describe him as "a sweet boy"; teachers "look out" for him; has a learning disability.

Stepfather: strict disciplinarian, favors his two biological sons.

Mother: doesn't interfere with her husband's discipline of Ricky.

RECENT INCIDENT

One day the teacher notices that when Ricky sits down at his desk he doesn't remove his backpack. The teacher suggests he remove his backpack so he can do his work. Ricky tells the teacher he can't take it off or he will get in trouble. She questions Ricky: "What do you mean you're going to get in trouble, Ricky?" "My dad said I had to wear it all day because I'm bad," he replies. The teacher smiles and says, "OK, but if you change your mind, I won't tell your dad."

By recess Ricky is still wearing his backpack. The school counselor walks by and noticed Ricky wearing his backpack on the playground. She asks the teacher what's going on. She relates Ricky's explanation. The counselor suggests that the teacher send Ricky to her office to see her.

When the counselor meets with Ricky, he explains that his dad told him he had to wear the backpack all day because he had wet his bed. The counselor asks Ricky if she may look in his backpack and see what's inside. Upon opening the backpack, the counselor finds 10 bricks inside. She asks Ricky if his dad put the bricks in his backpack. He responds, "Yes." She asks, "Ricky, when did your dad do this?" Ricky replies, "This morning when my mom told my dad that my bed was wet. My dad put the bricks in my backpack, and then I had to wear it at home and stay on my knees until it was time to go to the bus stop."

The counselor reports the incident to the building principal. The principal says it's unfortunate, but parents do have a right to punish their children. The counselor suggests that the incident be reported to Child Protective Services. The principal disagrees. Later that day the counselor does report the matter to Child Protective Services. An official there says CPS will check into it, but it doesn't sound all that serious, and it will take a few days.

CURRENT STATUS

The next day, Ricky is punished again for wetting his bed. This time, his stepfather makes Ricky walk to the bus stop wearing only his shirt, backpack, shoes, and underwear. He isn't allowed to wear his jeans. On the way to the bus stop, Ricky sees an oncoming car, jumps in front of it, and is hit and killed. Police rule the 4th-grader's death a suicide.

What are the symptoms?
What are the possible causes?
What could have been done that might have prevented this tragedy?

What resources do you think are present in the family, in the student, and in the school officials? Write **yes** if the resource is present, a **no** if it's missing, and a question mark (**?**) if you aren't sure.

RESOURCE	FAMILY	STUDENT	ADMINISTRATORS
Financial			
Emotional			
Mental			
Physical			
Support systems			
Relationships/role models			
Knowledge of boy code			

What is the parenting style of the stepfather?
    ___ Brick-wall   ___ Jellyfish   ___ Backbone

What is the parenting style of Ricky's mother?
    ___ Brick-wall   ___ Jellyfish   ___ Backbone

Which voice does each of the following use?

Stepfather: ___Parent   ___Child   ___Adult

Principal: ___Parent   ___Child   ___Adult

Counselor: ___Parent   ___Child   ___Adult

What are the symptoms and causes in the current situation?

What could school officials have done to help prevent this tragedy?

What should school personnel do, if anything, about the other two boys in the family, Ricky's two half-brothers?

SCENARIO #5: HANK

BACKGROUND

Hank: age 16, 9th grade, second year as 9th-grader, also repeated 8th grade, has girlfriend in 9th grade.

Mother: school counselor in neighboring school district.

Father: owns small business.

Mr. Ferguson: 20 years of teaching experience.

RECENT INCIDENT

On the way to school Hank's girlfriend informs him that she doesn't want to date him anymore. She isn't going to be his girlfriend any longer. Hank argues with her until the bell rings, and it's time for class. Hank goes to his first-period class and asks the teacher if he can go to his locker and get a book. The teacher allows him to go. Hank leaves the classroom and goes directly to the gym where his girlfriend is.

He looks in the gym, sees his girlfriend, and motions to her to come to the door. She complies. The physical education teacher is on the opposite end of the gym. As the girl approaches the door, Hank begins yelling at her: "You can't break up with me, you bitch!" The PE teacher begins working her way toward the door. As she approaches, Hank continues to yell at the girl. The teacher tells Hank that he needs to leave and asks the girl to return to class. Hank begins yelling obscenities at the teacher.

Mr. Ferguson's classroom is next door to the gym. He hears the commotion and comes out into the hall to see what's going on. Mr. Ferguson, a teacher with 20 years of experience, knows Hank and has had more than his share of incidents with him. Mr. Ferguson tells him to calm down and stop yelling. Hank yells back at him, then turns around to again address the girl. Mr. Ferguson puts his hand on Hank's arm and tries to turn him around and get his attention. Hank jerks his arm away, causing his hand to come into contact with the side of Mr. Ferguson's face. Mr. Ferguson tries to pin Hank's arms to his side. Hank breaks loose and begins to swing at Mr. Ferguson. The teacher blocks the swing and hits Hank on the side of the head. Within 30 seconds, the lives of a longtime respected teacher and a student have been altered. Security officers arrive. Hank is taken off campus by the police, handcuffed, and Mr. Ferguson faces a preliminary charge of assaulting a minor.

The principal contacts the father to notify him of the incident. The father says he hopes nothing happens to the teacher because he knows Hank has a temper. Mr. Ferguson is suspended with pay, pending completion of an investigation of the incident.

Later that day Hank is released to his parents. Hank is expelled from school, and he and his parents are told that Hank is not to set foot on campus until the hearing is completed. That afternoon Hank is left at home, and the parents return to their jobs. Hank leaves the house and returns to campus to find his ex-girlfriend. Hank is again apprehended by a school official, and the police are again called.

CURRENT STATUS

Administrative personnel conducting the investigation determine that Mr. Ferguson did indeed hit Hank. They also conclude that Hank was very angry, out of control, and tried to hit Mr. Ferguson. Two days following the incident, Hank's parents decide that Mr. Ferguson should be punished for what he did to their son and file assault charges with the police. Administrative personnel, following district policy, recommend that the teacher be suspended for hitting a student. The school board rules against the administration's recommendation, saying that Mr. Ferguson was only defending himself and that Hank was at fault.

What are the symptoms?

What are the possible causes?

What could have been done that might have prevented this situation?

What resources do you think are present in the family, in the student, and in the teacher? Write **yes** if the resource is present, a **no** if it's missing, and a question mark (**?**) if you aren't sure.

RESOURCE	FAMILY	TEACHER	STUDENT
Financial			
Emotional			
Mental			
Physical			
Support systems			
Relationships/role models			
Knowledge of boy code			

What is the parenting style of the parents?
        ___ Brick-wall   ___ Jellyfish   ___ Backbone

What is the teaching style of Mr. Ferguson?
        ___ Brick-wall   ___ Jellyfish   ___ Backbone

Which voice does each of the following use?

Parent(s):   ___Parent   ___Child   ___Adult

Mr. Ferguson: ___Parent   ___Child   ___Adult

Hank: ___Parent   ___Child   ___Adult

What are the symptoms and causes in the current situation?

What could school officials have done to help prevent this situation?

What recommendations would you have for Hank's parents?

What are your predictions concerning Hank's future? Is there anything school officials should be doing to alter Hank's course?

SCENARIO #6: BILL

BACKGROUND

Bill: age 11, 6th grade, known to be nice boy and good student who is very quiet, no disciplinary record, two younger sisters.

Father: employed in school district as athletic trainer at high school; attends church regularly; his church teaches that he is "head of his family," and his wife is his helpmate.

Mother: employed as secretary in school district.

Assistant principal: age 58, divorced, mother of two boys and one girl, two of her children are in college, longtime employee of school district.

Principal: age 55, first year as principal of current school, eight years of experience as administrator in another school district.

RECENT INCIDENT

Bill enters the school at 7:30 a.m. accompanied by his father. The father walks up to the assistant principal and asks if he could meet with her. She agrees, and Bill and his father enter her office. After talking with them briefly, the assistant principal summons the principal into the conference.

The father explains to the principal and the assistant principal, with Bill present, that he needs their help with his son. He explains that he has been having problems with the boy, and this morning "he crossed the line." He goes on to explain, "This morning Bill talked back to my wife, and that is totally unacceptable." Bill doesn't interrupt, remains silent, and looks down at the floor. Bill's dad continues to explain how difficult it has been raising Bill: "He has a smart mouth. I don't know why he can't be more like his sisters. They never give us a minute's trouble. We have just about broken him of leaving things on the floor in his room. He at least now puts his dirty clothes in the wash, and we have just about broken him of having feces stains on his underwear."

After Bill is excused to go to class, the father continues to talk another 15 minutes about the rudeness of his son toward his wife and wants the school to be aware of it and help him discipline Bill. The principal and assistant principal listen. Finally the father says he has to get to the high school. The principal walks him to the door. Upon leaving, the father turns to the principal and says, "You know, boys are just so much harder to raise than girls." The principal returns to the assistant principal's office and asks if she knew Bill's father. "Yes," she replied. "He graduated from our high school, and he has been the athletic trainer for several years. Everyone knows he's a nut case."

CURRENT STATUS

Later that day the principal asks Bill to come to his office. Upon talking with Bill privately, the principal apologizes to him for having to sit through the conference in which his father shared such personal and private information with him and the assistant principal. He also assures Bill that the information will not be shared with anyone else. He asks Bill what kind of punishment his father usually gives him. He explains that his dad hits him really hard with a belt. He adds that his father never hits his sisters. "They get away with everything. It's always my fault. I hate them."

"Bill, do you have a friend that you talk to?" the principal asks. After thinking for a moment, Bill replies, "My dog is my best friend. I talk to him. We go for long walks together when my dad isn't around. They don't like my dog." The principal and Bill talk about their mutual love for dogs and how they will love you even when you have a bad day. "I have some videos on how to train a dog. Would you like to take a look at them? They're pretty good," the principal comments. "Yeah, that would be neat," Bill replies. The principal continues, "You know, I have a couple of dogs, and I have competed with them in dog shows. Have you ever watched a dog show?" Answers Bill: "I saw one on TV once."

The principal finally gets Bill at a comfort level that he decides to return to the issue of his father hitting him. Bill explains that his dad swings his belt like a whip, hitting him all over his body. He says his dad doesn't do that as much as he used to when he was younger. He explains to the principal that he never cries. The principal asks him if that makes his dad angry. He said, "Yeah, it makes him real mad when I don't cry." The principal discusses with Bill the pros and cons of crying.

After listening to Bill's perception of the situation, the principal realizes there isn't justification for calling Child Protective Services, though he feels that the father's approach to discipline is inappropriate. He offers Bill the following advice:

- ◆ "You might want to think about wearing layered clothing, even in the summer. That way when your dad does hit you, it won't hurt as much."

- "Always have a wallet in your back pocket. That will help."

- "If you cry when he's hitting you, he will probably stop sooner."

- "You have to finish high school. That means you have to stay at home, even though there are things you don't like. You have to be smarter than your dad. Always be nice to your mom, especially around your dad."

The principal asks Bill if he will come see him the next time his dad hits him. Bill agrees. The principal brings the dog-training tapes to Bill the next day. He also let Bill's mom know that he gave them to Bill and compliments her on having such a nice young man. And he mentions that it is good for Bill to have a dog to play with. The mother agrees and thanks the principal for his comments.

What are the symptoms?
What are the possible causes?
What do school officials need to watch for?
What interventions could the school provide?

What resources do you think are present in the family, in the student, and in the administrators? Write **yes** if the resource is present, a **no** if it's missing, and a question mark (**?**) if you aren't sure.

RESOURCE	FAMILY	STUDENT	ADMINISTRATORS
Financial			
Emotional			
Mental			
Physical			
Support systems			
Relationships/role models			
Knowledge of boy code			

What is the parenting style of the parents?
___ Brick-wall   ___ Jellyfish   ___ Backbone

What is the administrative style of the assistant principal?
        ___ Brick-wall   ___ Jellyfish   ___ Backbone

What is the administrative style of the principal?
        ___ Brick-wall   ___ Jellyfish   ___ Backbone

Which voice does each of the following use?

Parent: ___Parent   ___Child   ___Adult

Administrators: ___Parent   ___Child   ___Adult

Bill: ___Parent   ___Child   ___Adult

What are the symptoms and causes in the current situation?

What would you say to the father?

What are your predictions concerning Bill's future? Is there anything the school should be doing to alter Bill's future?

What words of advice would you offer Bill?

Do you think school personnel would have handled this situation differently if Bill's parents had not been employees in the school district?

What's Underneath?

Student behavior is symptomatic. When school officials react only to what they see and hear, the real causes for the behavior often go unaddressed. When school personnel find themselves only enforcing the rules according to policy

without trying to get at the causes and then intervene, they have just crossed the line between education and law enforcement. School is for the purpose of educating. Behavior and student discipline are part of an educational process. Behavior must be taught. To do that, school officials must spend time and energy to get at the root causes of the behavior if they are to be effective change agents of behavior. It isn't easy, to be sure. On the surface, the iceberg may not appear large; but underneath the water, what cannot be seen is often huge. The "Titanic" didn't sink because of what was above the water.

Discussion of Scenarios

Scenario #1: José

José's family has some financial resources. What the family is missing are the emotional resources. José has been a problem to the parents his entire life. As jellyfish parents, they taught their son to be manipulative. They spent much of their time in his early years rescuing him from his problems. As a result, José has very little if any sense of who he is, and he has no confidence in his ability to solve his own problems. José is in pain. Not having the opportunity to develop the words to express his own ideas, thoughts, and feelings, José is an angry young man. He is lost in his own emotional abyss. José has no nurturing role models, no support system, and he's a classic example of the boy code. He keeps everything to himself. José's teacher is a brick-wall teacher and wants José out of her class. If José is out of sight, he's out of mind. As a result of José's family life, his grades reflect that he is lacking some basic skills. Learning cannot take place when a student comes to class angry.

Scenario #2: Matthew

Matthew's journey has just begun. His teacher is looking for simple solutions. She wants compliance and is relying on the stepfather to help her out. Though she may have no knowledge of the stepfather's disciplinary strategies, she has chosen to take the path of least resistance. It's easier to have the stepfather fix the situation than for her to deal with it in the classroom. Matthew is in pain. He is receiving harsh lessons in the boy code. Through the actions of his stepfather, he is being taught what being a "real boy" is about; if you need training wheels to ride a bike, you're a wimp. By removing the training wheels and forcing Matthew to experience his emotional pain and shame alone, the stepfather is teaching Matthew to bury his pain and learn not to talk about his feelings, ideas, and thoughts. The only feelings that count are the shame the stepfather feels about what others might think about the developmental level of his step-son. The mother's lack of interference on behalf of her son only reinforces the message that Matthew is inadequate. Matthew has plenty of financial resources. The emotional resources, however, are lacking in the home environment. Matthew's mother is a jellyfish parent and his stepfather is a brick-wall parent. Matthew certainly has the mental resources, as do the mother and the stepfather, but those resources are of no use without the emotional resources.

Matthew has a limited support system. Whatever he does or doesn't do in school will be reported to the stepfather. Matthew is a disaster in the making. As he gets older he will only become angrier, more disruptive in school. When Matthew is 15, the stepfather almost certainly won't be there for him. His best hope is that his biological father stays engaged in his life and becomes a positive force. The fact that the stepfather has social status in the community and has strong financial resources reduces the probability that the bio-father could become the support system Matthew needs.

Scenario #3: Adam

Adam has no resources. His grandparents may love him, but they have limited financial resources. Adam doesn't understand the boy code nor does he understand the world around him. Adam is a lonely, isolated young man who just wants to have a friend. His mother is an inappropriate role model for him. His grandmother appears to be unable to help him. Adam's lack of emotional resources certainly will take its toll on his academic performance. His grandmother is probably a jellyfish in her parenting style, trying to make Adam happy as a means of apologizing for her daughter's behavior and lifestyle. Adam has the potential of becoming even angrier and more isolated over time. He has no real role models and almost no support system.

SCENARIO #4: RICKY

Ricky is a young man who has fallen through the cracks of the system. All the warning signs were there:

- He was overweight.
- He had learning problems (but no one was talking with Ricky).
- His home life was filled with an angry, brick-wall stepfather who heaped guilt and shame on Ricky.
- He had no words and no one to turn to.

The school's lack of attention to Ricky's problems was masked by Ricky's "sweetness." How could a child so sweet have a problem? Ricky's lack of language, connected to his possible disability, just further compounded the situation. Ricky's mother was a jellyfish parent who was probably afraid of her brick-wall husband. The Rickys of the world are the silent criers. If no one is listening to the non-verbal cues, he goes unheard and self-destructs one way or another.

SCENARIO #5: HANK

Hank's parents are jellyfish parents. They are too busy to deal with their son's emotional needs. Hank is angry and has no emotional resources and no support systems. His conflict with his girlfriend just underscores the significance of his lack of support systems. His girlfriend had become his hope — maybe his last hope. She was his emotional resource and his support system. When she broke up with him, his world literally fell apart. The teacher in the incident also missed Hank's cry for help. The school has focused on Hank's lack of academic progress. Students who repeatedly fail are rarely seen as students who need intense, consistent support. Instead they are seen as students who have problems, and most school officials tend to assume the problems can't be fixed. Hank is alone, angry, and without resources from the school or his parents. Hank's journey has just begun. When he can drop out of school, he will. Without someone becoming seriously interested in helping Hank, he will almost certainly self-destruct. The school board's response to the teacher's actions only underscores the fact that the Hanks of the world are bad kids. While it may appear that the only one who loses is Hank, the fact is everyone loses when a human being of great potential gets forever lost in the abyss.

SCENARIO #6: BILL

Bill is a boy trapped in fear that will turn to anger without someone taking an interest in him. His silence in school, good grades, and aloneness will probably not be seen as a problem. Bill will survive school, but his anger toward his father is unpredictable. Bill has learned shame from his father. His father is a brick-wall parent who has no time or patience to listen to his son. He expects total compliance, and his son has very few rights. The fact that he sees his son insulting his wife, as opposed to Bill insulting his mother, sets Bill up to also distrust women and to see them as weak individuals.

Although Bill's father has the financial resources, his emotional resources are lacking. The parents and Bill have the mental resources, but Bill doesn't appear to have much of a support system or many role models, though he may find some of this from others at his church. The principal and assistant principal may be the best hope for Bill, who likely will never be able to live up to his father's "boy code" expectations. Bill's fate might be to continue working hard in school, hoping to meet the expectations of his father and somehow stay in his good graces, or he could become even angrier and lash back at his father when he gets older. This may include physical altercations. Bill is also a candidate for participating in dangerous, risky activities just to hurt his father.

> **Whatever a boy's genetic tendencies might be,
> the people with whom a boy interacts on a daily basis
> shape his moral development.
> When the resources are missing,
> we must look for ways of providing them.**

Chapter 12

Batter Up!

> *"His environment triggers anger and self-hatred."*
>
> —The Emotional Abyss
> p. 27

I Will Believe in You

No matter what you've done ...
I will believe in you.
No matter what has happened to you ...
I will believe in you.
No matter if you are rich or poor ...
I will believe in you.
No matter if your mom or dad is in jail ...
I will believe in you.
No matter what other teachers say ...
I will believe in you.
No matter what your brother or sister did ...
I will believe in you.
No matter where you live ...
I will believe in you.

AND

I will believe in you
until such time as
you can begin to believe in yourself!

—Adapted from
Mamie McCullough
Mamie McCullough & Associates
Dallas, TX
mamie@mamie.com

Chapter 12

Batter Up!

School personnel and parents must come together to help our boys. Myths still prevail and will continue to prevail until adults, especially men, make a conscious choice to work with boys in dispelling these myths. Myths eventually destroy people in that they promote one group as superior over another. They also set up unrealistic and unattainable expectations. Here are some of the myths that are most damaging to boys:

- ◆ Big boys don't cry.
- ◆ Being big and strong is manly.
- ◆ Drinking beer and getting drunk is a "guy thing."
- ◆ Being sexually active is a sign of manhood.
- ◆ Cursing/cussing is a sign of being grown-up.
- ◆ If you can't or won't fight, you're a wimp, wuss, etc.
- ◆ If you're straight, you're a man; if you're gay you're not a "real man."
- ◆ Getting good grades is a girl thing.
- ◆ To be a school boy, geek, or nerd isn't cool.
- ◆ The arts are for girls, sissies, and gays.
- ◆ Sharing thoughts and especially feelings is a girl thing.
- ◆ Real boys don't need help and don't ask for help.
- ◆ Real men don't ask for directions.
- ◆ Opting not to take certain risks means you're a wimp.
- ◆ If you are ridiculed and humiliated, you must be able to take it like a man.
- ◆ If you aren't involved in sports and good at them, you aren't a real guy.

- If you spend a lot of time with girls, without having sex with them, you're a fag.
- Liking clothes and being neat is a girl thing.
- Boys don't diet or eat salads.
- Boys must always win, especially when competing with girls.
- Never tell anyone if you're being teased, bullied, or hazed; guys don't snitch or rat on other guys.
- Boys and men don't do housework.
- Men have to make more money than women.
- Boys must be taller and smarter than the girls they date.
- Children need their mom more than they need their dad.

These myths are perpetuated in the Western culture through the media, peer groups, and family structures. As long as the media effectively sell whatever they have to sell, things probably won't change. To counteract this dynamic, boys need a little (and sometimes more than a little) help in the school and at home.

WHAT CAN PARENTS AND SCHOOL PERSONNEL DO?

1. As parents and school personnel, we must become more knowledgeable about boys. What behaviors are normal? Although boys move around more, not all boys need Ritalin for that movement. Teachers must take into account a boy's need for movement when planning classroom lessons.

2. Talk with boys about their feelings. Listen to them. Practice using action language to get boys to talk. Parents must initiate conversation and engage their sons in activities requiring action. That action may be sports, or it may be painting or playing the piano. It's here that parents must ask questions and **listen,** including listening to the non-verbals.

3. Don't judge. Listen. Using an adult voice allows boys to develop their own adult voice.

4. Implement a backbone style of teaching and mentoring, both as school personnel and as parents.

5. Talk with boys about what they hear and watch on television, video games, and the Internet. Ask the **what,** the **why,** and the **how** that is behind the TV shows and commercials.

6. Talk with boys about teasing, taunting, bullying. Let them know that it's wrong to ridicule and display a power position — physically or psychologically — over someone who appears different or vulnerable.

7. Talk with boys about "the boy code." Let them know what they're going to experience before they experience it. Talk with them about peers who won't like or accept them for being smart — and for liking or disliking certain things. Let them know that you're there to support them.

8. School personnel need to be ready to supply resources that some boys are lacking in the home, particularly for boys from poverty. When there's little or no support system at home, school officials and teachers are urged to look for ways they can help provide that support system.

9. Help boys develop an emotional vocabulary so they have the ability to articulate what is going on with them instead of simply acting out through overt behaviors.

10. Let boys know there's more than one way to be a guy. Girls are no less feminine because they play basketball or softball. Boys are no less masculine because they like to play chess, paint, or dance.

11. Look for signs of boys in pain:

    ♦ Acting depressed.

    ♦ Missing school.

    ♦ Not talking.

    ♦ Fighting.

    ♦ Changing their eating habits.

    ♦ Spending more and more time alone.

    ♦ Seeking out a new group of friends.

    ♦ Having sudden outbursts of anger.

    ♦ Becoming manipulative.

    ♦ Lying.

    ♦ Experiencing changes in grades.

    ♦ Becoming more secretive.

    Remember, these are symptoms, not causes.

12. As an adult, and especially as a man, don't be afraid to share your feelings. Sharing one's own feelings is a validation of those feelings that boys also may be experiencing. To have emotions is human; to be able to name one's emotions is liberating.

13. Parents should insist that restrooms and locker rooms at school be well-supervised. Any overnight trips or sports camps also must have good adult supervision, especially at night.

14. Parents and school personnel should encourage boys to participate in extracurricular activities sponsored by teachers who model dignity and respect and who know the importance of building positive relationships with boys.

15. Avoid playing games that require boys to be chosen — by other boys, by girls, or by adults. Being chosen last sets the stage for ridicule and being labeled a loser.

16. Provide role models of excellence for boys who come out of poverty, preferably using males who have survived adverse circumstances themselves.

17. School administrators and parent/teacher organizations should provide programs or workshops for parents on raising boys. Develop a professional library that is available to parents and teachers.

18. Utilizing well-trained counselors is essential.

19. School districts must develop policies and administrative regulations that require students to go through a process to get at the root causes of behavior rather than just punishing the symptoms.

20. Schools would do well to provide opportunities for boys to talk with other boys under the supervision of a nurturing, adult male. Help young men to develop a feeling vocabulary, along with empathy for others.

Masculinity is not defined by occupation, hobbies, or interests, but by how a male honors himself and others. The empathy he has will define his conscience, his sense of right and wrong. His boundaries will define his personal code of ethics and sense of personal integrity. He will have the words to connect with his family, his friends, his community, and himself.

HEAR MY CRY!

I am in your classrooms.
I am in your alternative schools and boot camps.
I am in special education and in your gifted classes.
I am in your detention halls and your office.
Hear my cry.

I am in your home.
I am the boy next door.
I am in your workplace.
I am your son, stepson, grandson, nephew, or friend.
Hear my cry.

My tears are behind my silence.
My tears are masked in my pain of anger.
My tears are buried in my shame.
My tears have no words.
I am alone in the silence of the night.
Hear my cry!

—*Paul D. Slocumb*, Ed.D.

Author's Afterword

Between 1976 and 1997
parents and stepparents
murdered nearly 11,000 children.
Mothers and stepmothers committed
about half of these child murders.
Sons and stepsons accounted for 52%
of those killed by mothers
and 57% of those killed by fathers.
Mothers were responsible
for a higher share of children
killed during infancy,
while fathers were more likely
to have been responsible for
the murders of children age 8 or older.

Greenfeld & Snell, 1999

Author's Afterword

*T*his book is about boys. However, much of the information in this book is also applicable to girls. In fact, the path that all too many boys have taken should serve as a warning for girls as more and more of them enter the workforce, and increasing numbers become the sole breadwinner for their families. If females buy in to some of the popular images now being projected for women through media, they too will enter into their own *emotional abyss*. The image of corporate America was created primarily by males. What is the fate of the next generation of children if women also subscribe to a philosophy that "Big girls don't cry"? If women embrace the idea that they must play by the rules of the "man's world," what will be lost?

Certainly women have the rights, the skills, and the abilities to function productively in corporate America. It's not a man's world; it's a humans' world. Women may be the hope for a new paradigm in the Western world. But if they disconnect emotionally from their families and communities in their quest to "get ahead," then everyone loses.

This book is about helping young boys become responsible and emotionally engaged adults who are connected to their families, neighborhoods, and communities. It is about the myths of boyhood that have been created by generations and cultures that have come before them. The cost for endorsing these myths is alarming:

- Increased numbers of males in prison.
- Fewer fathers actively involved in the raising of their children.

- Fewer boys than girls pursuing college degrees
- Far more boys than girls in special education, alternative schools, and the principal's office.
- Increased male-on-male violence, especially among younger boys.
- Boys lacking the skills necessary to be successful in personal relationships.

If girls and young women feel they too must be a "Charlie's Angel," a superhero who leaps tall buildings in a single bound and kick-boxes male villains into oblivion, one who competes and wins at all cost, one who plays by the rules *men* created for the "man's world," then who will be left to nurture the next generation of children? The ultimate price may be a generation of boys *and* girls who have little empathy or conscience.

Not possible? Today's statistics for females may not be as shocking as they are for males, but the numbers are growing. Examine the data.

- Increasing numbers of females in prison.
- Increasing numbers of females addicted to drugs and alcohol.
- Females becoming sexually active at younger ages.
- More grandparents raising their grandchildren.

The challenge regarding *both* genders lies ahead.

Appendix

Data collected from
1,000 high schools in 26 states
reveal a "deep-seated malaise
about learning among the boys.
While 84% of girls in the survey
said it was important to continue
their education beyond high school,
only 67% of the boys agreed."

The number of women receiving degrees
is rising faster than for men.
The percentage of increase in degrees
awarded from 1990 to 2000:

	Women	Men
Bachelor's:	26%	8%
Master's:	55%	25%
Doctorate:	42%	3%

"Boys' Academic Slide," 2003

APPENDIX A

Prisoners Under the Jurisdiction of State or Federal Correctional Authorities, by Sex, December 31, 2012 and 2013

	2012			2013			Percent change, 2012–2013		
Jurisdiction	Total	Male	Female	Total	Male	Female	Total	Male	Female
U.S. total[a,b]	1,570,397	1,461,625	108,772	1,574,741	1,463,454	111,287	0.3%	0.1%	2.3%
Federal[c]	217,815	203,766	14,049	215,866	201,697	14,169	-0.9%	-1.0%	0.9%
State[a,b]	1,352,582	1,257,859	94,723	1,358,875	1,261,757	97,118	0.5%	0.3%	2.5%

Source: Carson, E. A. (2014, September). Prisoners in 2013 [NCJ 247282]. Bureau of Justice Statistics.

Note: Jurisdiction refers to the legal authority of state or federal correctional officials over a prisoner, regardless of where the prisoner is held. As of December 31, 2001, sentenced felons from the District of Columbia were the responsibility of the Federal Bureau of Prisons.
[a]Includes imputed counts for Nevada. See Methodology for imputation strategy.
[b]Alaska did not submit sex-specific jurisdiction counts to NPS in 2013. See Methodology.
[c]Includes inmates held in nonsecure privately operated community corrections facilities and juveniles held in contract facilities.

- An estimated 1,574,700 people were incarcerated on December 31, 2013.

- 1.2% of adult males and 0.9% of males of all ages were incarcerated in state or federal prisons on December 31, 2013.

- The imprisonment rate decreased for adult males from 1,201 per 100,000 in 2012 to 1,191 per 100,000 in 2013.

- The imprisonment rate increased for adult females by 2% from 2012 to 2013.

Sentenced Prisoners Under the Jurisdiction of State or Federal Correctional Authorities, by Age, Sex, Race, and Hispanic Origin, December 31, 2013

Age	Male						Female				
	Total[a]	Total male[a,b]	White[c]	Black[c]	Hispanic	Other[b,c]	Total female[a,b]	White[c]	Black[c]	Hispanic	Other[b,c]
Total[d]	100%	100%	100%	100%	100%	100%	100%	100%	100%	100%	100%
18–19	1.0%	1.1%	0.6%	1.3%	1.3%	1.1%	0.6%	0.4%	0.9%	1.1%	0.8%
20–24	11.4	11.4	8.6	13.0	12.7	12.4	10.2	8.7	11.3	12.5	10.9
25–29	15.3	15.2	13.2	15.5	17.2	17.2	17.3	16.6	16.5	20.5	20.2
30–34	16.7	16.6	15.1	16.8	18.6	17.9	18.3	18.4	16.9	19.9	21.0
35–39	13.9	13.9	12.7	14.1	15.5	14.2	14.4	14.5	13.9	14.8	14.3
40–44	12.5	12.5	13.0	12.2	12.3	12.4	13.2	13.7	13.4	11.4	11.8
45–49	10.8	10.8	12.2	10.5	9.1	9.5	11.3	11.7	12.1	9.1	9.2
50–54	8.4	8.5	10.4	8.2	6.3	7.0	7.7	8.2	7.8	5.7	6.7
55–59	4.9	5.0	6.4	4.6	3.6	4.0	3.8	3.9	4.3	2.8	3.4
60–64	2.5	2.6	3.7	2.1	1.8	2.1	1.7	2.0	1.7	1.1	1.7
65 or older	2.1	2.2	3.8	1.2	1.4	1.8	1.2	1.4	0.9	1.1	0.8
Total number of sentenced prisoners	1,516,879	1,412,745	454,100	526,000	314,600	118,100	104,134	51,500	23,100	17,600	11,900

Note: Jurisdiction refers to the legal authority of state or federal correctional officials over a prisoner, regardless of where the prisoner is held. Counts are based on prisoners with sentences of more than a year under the jurisdiction of state or federal correctional officials. Nevada did not submit 2013 data to NPS and Alaska did not submit sex-specific counts or sentence length data in 2013. See Methodology for imputation strategy.
[a]Detail may not sum to total due to rounding, inclusion of inmates age 17 or younger in the total count, and missing race or Hispanic origin data.
[b]Includes American Indians, Alaska Natives, Asians, Native Hawaiians, Pacific Islanders, persons of two or more races, or additional racial categories in reporting information systems.
[c]Excludes persons of Hispanic or Latino orgin.
[d]Includes persons age 17 or younger.
Sources: Bureau of Justice Statistics, National Prisoner Statistics Program, 2013; Federal Justice Statistics Program, 2012–2013; National Corrections Reporting Program, 2012; and Survey of Inmates in State and Federal Correctional Facilities, 2004.
Source: Carson, E. A. (2014, September). Prisoners in 2013 [NCJ 247282]. Bureau of Justice Statistics.

GENDER, RACE, AND AGE CHARACTERISTICS

◆ 17% of all inmates were ages 30–34, and an estimated 2% were age 65 or older in 2013.

◆ 58% of male inmates and 61% of female inmates were age 39 or younger.

◆ Among males, white prisoners were generally older than black or Hispanic prisoners. An estimated 17,300 inmates age 65 or older (54%) were white males.

◆ Approximately 3% of black male U.S. residents of all ages were imprisoned on December 31, 2013, compared to 1% of Hispanic males and 0.5% of white males.

- There were fewer black females in state or federal prison in 2013 than in 2012; however, black females were imprisoned at more than twice the rate of white females.

- Black males had higher imprisonment rates across all age groups than all other races.

- Black males (ages 25–39), were imprisoned at rates at least 2.5 times greater than Hispanic males and 6 times greater than white males.

- For males ages 18–19, black males were more than 9 times more likely to be imprisoned than white males.

- Black females ages 18–19 were 5 times more likely to be imprisoned than white females.

Source: Carson, E. A. (2014, September). Prisoners in 2013 [NCJ 247282]. Bureau of Justice Statistics.

Estimated Percent of Sentenced Prisoners Under State Jurisdiction, by Offense and Sex, Race, and Hispanic Origin, December 31, 2012

Most serious offense	Total inmates[a]	Male	Female	White[b]	Black[b]	Hispanic	Other[a,b]
Total	100%	100%	100%	100%	100%	100%	100%
Violent	53.8%	55.0%	37.1%	49.3%	58.3%	59.9%	58.8%
Murder[c]	12.7	12.8	11.1	9.9	13.7	14.9	17.0
Manslaughter	1.3	1.3	2.5	1.6	1.0	1.2	1.9
Rape/sexual assault	12.2	13.0	2.3	17.0	8.0	13.2	12.6
Robbery	13.7	14.0	8.7	8.2	20.4	13.4	10.0
Aggravated or simple assault	10.7	10.8	8.9	9.3	11.5	13.6	13.2
Other violent	3.2	3.2	3.7	3.3	3.6	3.6	4.1
Property	18.8%	18.1%	28.2%	24.5%	16.0%	12.9%	17.3%
Burglary	9.9	10.2	6.9	12.0	9.4	8.0	8.6
Larceny-theft	3.7	3.3	9.1	5.2	3.2	1.9	3.3
Motor vehicle theft	0.9	0.9	0.8	1.2	0.5	1.0	1.6
Fraud	2.0	1.5	8.4	2.9	1.4	0.8	2.1
Other property	2.2	2.2	3.0	3.2	1.4	1.2	1.9
Drug	16.0%	15.4%	24.6%	14.0%	15.9%	15.1%	11.7%
Drug possession	3.7	3.5	6.7	4.0	4.0	4.2	3.7
Other drug[d]	12.2	11.8	17.9	10.0	11.9	11.0	8.0
Public-order[e]	10.7%	10.8%	8.9%	11.6%	9.5%	11.5%	11.5%
Other/unspecified[f]	0.8%	0.7%	1.2%	0.6%	0.3%	0.5%	0.7%
Total number of sentenced inmates	1,314,900	1,225,900	89,000	462,600	498,100	271,700	82,500

Note: Estimates are based on state prisoners with a sentence of more than a year under the jurisdiction of state correctional officials. Detail may not sum to total due to rounding and missing offense data. See Methodology.
[a]Includes American Indians, Alaska Natives, Asians, Native Hawaiians, Pacific Islanders, persons of two or more races, or additional racial categories in reporting information systems.
[b]Excludes persons of Hispanic or Latino origin and persons of two or more races.
[c]Includes nonnegligent manslaughter.
[d]Includes trafficking and other drug offenses.
[e]Includes weapons, drunk driving, and court offenses; commercialized vice, morals, and decency offenses; and liquor law violations and other public-order offenses.
[f]Includes juvenile offenses and other unspecified offense categories.

Sources: Bureau of Justice Statistics, National Prisoner Statistics Program and National Corrections Reporting Program, 2012; and Survey of Inmates in State Correctional Facilities, 2004.

If the current trend continues, approximately two million Americans will be under correctional supervision within a ten-year period. By 2020 the total probation, jail, prison, and parole population could reach 10,445,100.

CHARACTERISTICS OF JAIL INMATES

+ Thirty-one percent of jail inmates had grown up with a parent or guardian who abused alcohol or drugs.

+ About 12% had lived in a foster home or institution.

+ Forty-six percent had a family member who had been incarcerated.

+ More than 50% of the women in jail had been physically or sexually abused in the past, compared with more than 10% of the men.

+ More than half of all state prison inmates were violent offenders, while more than half of federal prisoners were drug offenders.

+ In 2012, 54% of inmates in state prisons were serving sentences for violent offenses, and 19% were convicted of property offenses.

+ More males (55%) were imprisoned for violent offenses than females (37%).

+ Drug offenders made up 16% of the total state prison population in 2012.

+ Prisoners who were serving time for drug offenses included 25% of female prisoners, compared to 15% of male prisoners.

Source: Carson, E. A. (2014, September). Prisoners in 2013 [NCJ 247282]. Bureau of Justice Statistics.

Estimated Number of Parents in State and Federal Prisons and Their Minor Children, by Inmate's Gender

	Total	Parents in state prison			Parents in federal prison[a]		
		Total	Male	Female	Total	Male	Female
Number of parents							
2007	809,800	686,000	627,800	58,200	123,800	116,400	7,400
2004[b]	754,900	644,100	592,300	51,800	110,800	104,200	6,600
1999	721,500	642,300	593,800	48,500	79,200	74,100	5,100
1997	649,500	587,000	544,100	42,900	62,500	58,500	4,000
1991	452,500	413,100	386,500	26,600	39,400	36,500	2,900
Number of minor children							
2007	1,706,600	1,427,500	1,296,500	131,000	279,100	262,700	16,400
2004[b]	1,590,100	1,340,300	1,223,700	116,600	249,800	235,200	14,600
1999[c]	1,515,200	1,338,900	1,223,400	115,500	176,300	165,700	10,600
1997[c]	1,362,900	1,223,800	1,121,400	102,400	139,100	130,800	8,300
1991[c]	945,600	860,300	802,300	58,000	85,100	79,200	5,900

Note: See Methodology for details about estimation methods.
[a]Estimates were based on the prisoner custody population in each year. The total custody population included inmates held in privately operated facilities and community corrections centers (30,379 in 2007; 24,768 in 2004; and 3,828 inmates in privately operated facilities in 1999). In 1991 and 1997, the number of inmates in these facilities was not known.
[b]Numbers were estimated based on the June 30, 2004, custody population in state (1,241,034) and federal (176,156) prisons.
[c]Estimates may not be comparable to previously published BJS reports. See Methodology for more detail.
Source: Glaze, L. E., & Maruschak, L. M. (2008). Parents in prison and their minor children. Bureau of Justice Statistics. Retrieved from http://www.bjs.gov/content/pub/pdf/pptmc.pdf

Estimated Number of Parents in State and Federal Prisons and Their Minor Children, by Inmate's Gender, Race, and Hispanic Origin, 2004 and 2007

	Male				Female			
	Total[a]	White[b]	Black[b]	Hispanic	Total[a]	White[b]	Black[b]	Hispanic
State inmates								
Number of parents 2007	627,800	197,800	262,400	127,600	58,200	29,000	16,100	8,800
2004[c]	592,300	189,800	279,500	113,100	51,800	23,300	19,000	8,200
Number of children 2007	1,296,500	373,400	577,900	263,500	131,000	60,000	39,600	22,900
2004[c]	1,223,700	358,000	611,600	233,000	116,600	47,900	45,700	21,000
Federal inmates								
Number of parents 2007	116,400	25,900	57,000	32,500	7,400	2,700	2,200	2,300
2004[c]	104,200	20,900	49,300	31,000	6,600	2,000	2,100	2,200
Number of children 2007	262,700	45,100	144,800	71,200	16,400	5,600	5,100	5,200
2004[c]	235,200	36,300	125,400	67,800	14,600	4,200	4,900	4,900

Note: See Methodology for estimation methods.
[a]Includes other races. Other races include American Indians, Alaska Natives, Asians, Native Hawaiians, other Pacific Islanders, and persons identifying two or more races.
[b]Excludes persons of Hispanic or Latino origin.
[c]Numbers were estimated based on the June 30, 2004 custody population in state (1,241,034) and federal (176,156) prisons.
Source: Glaze, L. E., & Maruschak, L. M. (2008). Parents in prison and their minor children. Bureau of Justice Statistics. Retrieved from http://www.bjs.gov/content/pub/pdf/pptmc.pdf

PARENTS IN PRISON AND THEIR MINOR CHILDREN

◆ Parents held in the nation's prisons midyear 2007: 52% of state inmates and 63% of federal inmates reported having an estimated 1,706,600 minor children, accounting for 2.3% of the U.S. resident population under the age of 18.

◆ As of July 1, 2007, black children (6.7%) were seven and a half times more likely than white children (0.9%) to have a parent in prison. Hispanic children (2.4%) were more than two and a half times more likely than white children to have a parent in prison.

◆ While growing up, 40% of parents in state prison reported living in a household that received public assistance, 14% reported living in a foster home, agency, or institution at some time during their youth, and 43% reported living with both parents most of the time.

◆ More than a third (34%) of parents in state prison reported that during their youth their parents or guardians had abused alcohol or drugs.

◆ Among parents in state prison, 9% reported homelessness in the year before arrest, 20% had a history of physical or sexual abuse, and 41% reported a current medical problem. Fifty-seven percent of parents in state prison met the criteria for a mental health problem, and 67% met the criteria for substance dependence or abuse.

◆ There was a 79% increase in the number of parents of minor children being incarcerated between 1991 and 2007.

◆ Since 1991 the number of children under age 18 with a mother in prison has more than doubled.

◆ More than a third of minor children with a parent in prison will turn 18 while their parent is in prison.

◆ In the month before their arrest, more than 40% of the mothers in state prison who had minor children were living in single-parent households.

◆ About 50% of parents in state prison provided the primary financial support for their minor children.

Source: "Survey of Inmates," (n.d.)

An estimated 12% of African-American males in their late 20s were in prison or jail in 2005. When total incarceration rates are estimated separately by age group, black males in their 20s and 30s are found to have very high rates relative to other groups. Among the nearly 2.2 million offenders incarcerated on June 30, 2005, an estimated 548,300 were black males between the ages of 20 and 39. Of black non-Hispanic males ages 25–29, 11.9% were in prison or jail, compared with 3.9% of Hispanic males and about 1.7% of white males in the same age group. In general, the incarceration rates for black males of all ages were five to seven times greater than those for white males in the same age groups.

Prisoners Under Jurisdiction of State or Federal Correctional Authorities by Region from Highest to Lowest: June 30, 2008

South	648,126	Alabama, Arkansas, Delaware, Florida, Georgia, Kentucky, Louisiana, Maryland, Mississippi, North Carolina, Oklahoma, South Carolina, Tennessee, Texas, Virginia, West Virginia
West	316,854	Alaska, Arizona, California, Colorado, Hawaii, Idaho, Montana, Nevada, New Mexico, Oregon, Utah, Washington, Wyoming
Midwest	265,342	Illinois, Indiana, Iowa, Kansas, Michigan, Minnesota, Missouri, Nebraska, North Dakota, Ohio, South Dakota, Wisconsin
Northeast	179,120	Connecticut, Maine, Massachusetts, New Hampshire, New Jersey, New York, Pennsylvania, Rhode Island, Vermont
State	1,409,442	
Federal	201,142	
U.S. total	1,610,584	

Source: West & Sabol, 2009

By geographic areas of the country as of June 30, 2008, the South had the highest prison rate. Of those southern states, Texas had the highest incarceration rate in the country and the second highest prison rate. The second highest prison rate was the West. Of those western states, California had the highest prison rate and second highest incarceration rate in the country. The Midwest had the third highest prison rate and the Northeast had the lowest.

LIFETIME LIKELIHOOD OF GOING TO STATE OR FEDERAL PRISON

- ◆ If recent incarceration rates remain unchanged, an estimated one of every 15 persons (6.6%percent) will serve time in a prison during their lifetime.
- ◆ Lifetime chances of a person going to prison are higher for:
    —men (11.3%) than for women (1.8%)
    —blacks (18.6%) and Hispanics (10%) than for whites (3.4%)

Based on current rates of first incarceration, an estimated 32% of black males will enter state or federal prison during their lifetime, compared with 17% of Hispanic males and 5.9% of white males.

APPENDIX B

SEEKING PROFESSIONAL HELP

School officials are often reluctant to recommend that parents seek professional help for their children. This reluctance is due in part to an overall lack of knowledge about the role of a school counselor and a psychologist. Many parents also are reluctant to accept the fact that their child may need help beyond what the school can offer. The following information can be used to assist school personnel in explaining the services of a licensed psychologist.

PSYCHOTHERAPY AND HOW TO OBTAIN TREATMENT: FREQUENTLY ASKED QUESTIONS

Sources: Janel H. Miller, Ph.D., Houston, TX
and
American Psychological Association Practice Directorate

WHAT IS PSYCHOTHERAPY?

Psychotherapy is a collaborative effort between a therapist and client to help develop healthier, more effective patterns of behavior through in-depth exploration of feelings and thoughts. Treatment varies, depending on the therapist's and client's personalities and the particular problems the client is experiencing. Many different methods may be used to deal with the problems the client wishes to address. In all cases, however, psychotherapy calls for active effort on the client's part. In order for therapy to be most successful, the client will need to work on things both during sessions and at home. Psychotherapists maintain confidentiality and answer questions regarding those rare circumstances when confidential information must be shared.

WHAT HAPPENS IN PSYCHOTHERAPY?

Psychotherapy has been demonstrated to have many benefits. Therapy leads to better relationships, solutions to specific problems, and significant reductions in feelings of distress. However, since therapy often involves discussing unpleasant aspects of one's life, clients may experience uncomfortable feelings such as sadness, guilt, anger, frustration, loneliness, and helplessness. Because therapy involves a large commitment, clients should be very careful about the therapist they select.

The first few sessions involve an evaluation of the client's needs. By the end of the evaluation, the therapist will be able to offer some initial impressions of what the work would include if the client decided to continue with therapy. A client's level of comfort is one of the most important factors in choosing a therapist and building a therapeutic relationship. The skill and credentials of the therapist are essential as well.

WHAT IS THE DIFFERENCE BETWEEN A PSYCHOLOGIST, COUNSELOR, SOCIAL WORKER, AND PSYCHIATRIST?

Psychologists spend an average of seven years in graduate education training and research before receiving a doctoral degree. As part of their professional training, they must complete a supervised clinical internship in a hospital or organized health setting and at least one year of post-doctoral supervised experience before they can practice independently in any healthcare arena.

Licensed professional counselors, marriage and family therapists, and clinical social workers possess a master's degree or doctorate in some form of counseling, with two or three years of academic work, supervised practicum experience, and a post-graduate supervised experience.

A psychiatrist has a general medical degree (usually four years) and a residency (another four years) specific to psychiatry. Psychiatrists usually deal with the pharmaceutical part of mental health, though some psychiatrists also provide psychotherapy.

WHO PAYS FOR THE TREATMENTS?

Many insurance companies provide coverage for psychotherapy. For clients who have private health insurance coverage (typically through an employer), the insurance company may help obtain these benefits. This also applies to persons enrolled in health maintenance organizations (HMOs), preferred provider organizations (PPOs), and other types of managed-care plans. Clients should find out how much the insurance company will reimburse for psychotherapy and what limitations on the use of benefits may apply. If the client is not covered by a private health insurance plan or employee assistance program (EAP), the client may decide to pay for the services out-of-pocket.

ARE THERE SOME OTHER OPTIONS FOR THOSE WHO CANNOT AFFORD TREATMENT?
Community mental health centers throughout the United States are another possible alternative for receiving services. Some state Medicaid programs for economically disadvantaged individuals also provide for limited psychotherapy.

Bibliography

Bibliography

American Psychological Association. (2013, November). Psychologists study media violence for harmful effects. Retrieved from http://www.apa.org/action/resources/research-in-action/protect.aspx

Anderson, C. A., & Bushman, B. J. (2002). The effects of media violence on society. *Science, 295,* 2378.

Average daily media use in the United States from 2010 to 2014 (in minutes). (2015). Retrieved from http://www.statista.com/statistics/270781/average-daily-media-use-in-the-us/

Baron-Cohen, S. (2003). *The essential difference: The truth about the male and female brain.* New York, NY: Basic Books.

Baron-Cohen, S., Lutchmaya, S., & Knickmeyer, R. (2004). *Prenatal testosterone in mind.* Cambridge, MA: MIT Press.

Borzelleca, D. (2012, February 16). The male-female ratio in college. *Forbes.* Retrieved from http://www.forbes.com/sites/ccap/2012/02/16/the-male-female-ratio-in-college/

Boys' academic slide calls for accelerated attention [Editorial]. (2003, December 22). *USA Today,* p. 17A. Retrieved from http://www.usatoday.com/news/opinion/editorials/2003-12-22-our-view_x.htm

Boys: Getting it right. Report on the inquiry into the education of boys. (2002). House of Representatives Standing Committee on Education and Training, The Parliament of the Commonwealth of Australia. Retrieved from http://www.aph.gov.au/house/committee/EDT/eofb/report/fullrpt.pdf

Boys project home. (n.d.) Retrieved from http://boysproject.net/index.html

Brill, R. (2000). *Emotional honesty and self-acceptance: Education strategies for preventing violence.* Philadelphia, PA: Xlibris.

Brown, C. B. (2002, September 30). Reality TV bites: Bracing for new season of bullies. *The Houston Chronicle,* p. 23A.

Bullies. (2009). Retrieved from http://www.drphil.com/shows/show/115

Bureau of Justice Statistics. (2010). Home page. Retrieved from http://bjs.ojp.usdoj.gov/

Carson, E. A. (2014, September). Prisoners in 2013 [NCJ 247282]. Bureau of Justice Statistics. Retrieved from http://www.bjs.gov/content/pub/pdf/p13.pdf

Children and families of the incarcerated fact sheet. (2014). National Resource Center on Children and Families of the Incarcerated. Retrieved from nrccfi.camden.rutgers.edu/files/nrccfi-fact-sheet-2014.pdf13.pdf

Coloroso, B. (2003). *The bully, the bullied, and the bystander.* New York, NY: Harper Resource.

Conlin, M. (2003, May 26). The new gender gap. *BusinessWeek,* 75–82.

Cox, A. J. (2006). *Boys of few words.* New York, NY: Guilford Press.

Diamond, J. (2001). Unwritten knowledge. *Nature, 410,* 521. doi:10.1038/35069154

Duggan, M., Ellison, N. B., Lampe, C., Lenhart, A., & Madden, M. (2015, January 9). Social media update 2014. Retrieved from http://www.pewinternet.org/2015/01/09/social-media-update-2014/

Dye, L. (2003, June 25). Study: Teens' minds wired for cheap thrills. Retrieved from http://abcnews.go.com/Technology/story?id=97605&page=1

Galley, M. (2002, January 23). Boys to men. *Education Week, 26–29.*

Gardner, H. (1993). *Frames of mind: The theory of multiple intelligences.* New York, NY: Basic Books.

Glaze, L. E., & Maruschak, L. M. (2008). Parents in prison and their minor children. Bureau of Justice Statistics Special Report NCJ 222984. Retrieved from http://bjs.ojp.usdoj.gov/content/pub/pdf/pptmc.pdf

Greenfeld, L. A., & Snell, T. L. (1999). Women offenders. Bureau of Justice Statistics Special Report NCJ 175688. Retrieved from http://bjs.ojp.usdoj.gov/content/pub/pdf/wo.pdf

Gurian, M. (1998). *A fine young man: What parents, mentors, and educators can do to shape adolescent boys into exceptional men.* New York, NY: Penguin Putnam.

Gurian, M. (1999). *The good son: Shaping the moral development of our boys and young men.* New York, NY: Jeremy P. Tarcher/Putnam.

Gurian, M. (2001). *Boys and girls learn differently: A guide for teachers and parents.* San Francisco, CA: Jossey-Bass.

Gurian, M., & Stevens, K. (2005). *The minds of boys: Saving our sons from falling behind in school and life.* San Francisco, CA: Jossey-Bass.

Harrison, P. M., & Beck, A. J. (2002). Prisoners in 2001. Bureau of Justice Statistics Bulletin NCJ 195189. Retrieved from http://bjs.ojp.usdoj.gov/content/pub/pdf/p01.pdf

Harrison, P. M., & Beck, A. J. (2005). Prisoners in 2004. Bureau of Justice Statistics Bulletin NCJ 210677. Retrieved from http://bjs.ojp.usdoj.gov/content/pub/pdf/p04.pdf

Hart, B., & Risley, T. (1995). *Meaningful differences in the everyday experience of young American children.* Baltimore, MD: Paul H. Brookes.

Healy, J. (1998). *Failure to connect.* New York, NY: Simon & Schuster.

Howard, P. J. (2000). *The owner's manual for the brain: Everyday applications from mind-brain research.* Atlanta, GA: Bard Press.

Johnson, J. G., Cohen, P., Smailes, E. M., Kasen, S., & Brook, J. S. (2002). Television viewing and aggressive behavior during adolescence and adulthood. *Science, 295,* 2468–2471. doi:10.1126/science.1062929

Joos, M. (1967). The styles of the five clocks. In R. D. Abraham & R. C. Troike (Eds.), *Language and cultural diversity in American education* (pp. 145–149). Englewood Cliffs, NJ: Prentice Hall.

Kant, G. (2013, April 1). Radical increase in kids prescribed Ritalin. WND. Retrieved from http://www.wnd.com/2013/04/radical-increase-in-kids-prescribed-ritalin/

Key facts at a glance: Correction populations. (2010). Retrieved from http://bjs.ojp.usdoj.gov/content/glance/tables/corr2tab.cfm

Kindlon, D., & Thompson, M. (1999). *Raising Cain.* New York, NY: Ballantine.

Kohn, D. (2003, May 25). The gender gap: Boys lagging. Retrieved from http://www.cbsnews.com/stories/2002/10/31/60minutes/main527678.shtml

McCullough, M. (n.d.). Welcome! Retrieved from http://mamie.com/index2.html

McGraw, P. (2003, June 15). Dr. Phil's "manual." *O, The Oprah Magazine, 4*(6), 46–50. Retrieved from http://www.oprah.com/omagazine/Dr-Phils-MANual/1

Model for tragedy. (2000, March 1). *The Houston Chronicle,* p. 1D.

Moir, A., & Jessel, D. (1992). *Brain sex: The real difference between men and women.* New York, NY: Delta.

Nerburn, K. (1999). *Letters to my son.* Novato, CA: New World Library.

Number of monthly active Facebook users in the United States and Canada as of 1st quarter 2015 (in millions). (2015). Retrieved from http://www.statista.com/statistics/ 247614/number-of-monthly-active-facebook-users-worldwide/

Number of subscribers to wireless carriers in the U.S. from 1st quarter 2013 to 3rd quarter 2014, by carrier (in millions). (2015). Retrieved from http://www.statista.com/statistics/283507/subscribers-to-top-wireless-carriers-in-the-us/

Olweus, D. (1993). *Bullying at school: What we know and what we can do.* Cambridge, MA: Blackwell.

Payne, R. K. (2002a). *Learning structures.* Highlands, TX: aha! Process.

Payne, R. K. (2002b). *Understanding learning.* Highlands, TX: aha! Process.

Payne, R. K. (2010). *Research-based strategies: Narrowing the achievement gap for under-resourced students.* Highlands, TX: aha! Process.

Payne, R. K. (2013). *A framework for understanding poverty: A cognitive approach.* Highlands, TX: aha! Process.

Pelzer, D. (1995). *A child called "It."* Deerfield Beach, FL: Health Communications.

Pelzer, D. (1997). *The lost boy.* Deerfield Beach, FL: Health Communications.

Pelzer, D. (1999). *A man named Dave.* New York, NY: Penguin Putnam.

Pleck, J., Sonenstein, F., Ku, L., & Burbridge, L. (1993). Masculinity ideology: Its impact on adolescent males' heterosexual relationships. *Journal of Social Issues, 49,* 11–29.

Pollack, W. (1998). *Real boys: Rescuing our sons from myths of boyhood.* New York, NY: Henry Holt.

Pollack, W. (2000). *Real boys' voices.* New York, NY: Random House.

Pollack, W., & Cushman, K. (2001). *Real boys workbook: The definitive guide to understanding and interacting with boys of all ages.* New York, NY: Villard Books.

Postman, N. (1985). *Amusing ourselves to death.* New York, NY: Penguin.

Postman, N. (1994). *The disappearance of childhood.* New York, NY: Vintage Books.

Postman, N. (1995). *The end of education.* New York, NY: Vintage Books.

Postman, N. (1999). *Building a bridge to the 18th century.* New York, NY: Vintage Books.

Robertson, L. A., McAnally, H. M., & Hancox, R. J. (2013). Childhood and adolescent television viewing and antisocial behavior in early adulthood. *Pediatrics, 131*(3), 439–446. doi:10.1542/peds. 2012-1582

Sabol, W. J., West, H. C., & Cooper, M. (2009). Prisoners in 2008. Bureau of Justice Statistics Bulletin NCJ 228417. Retrieved from http://bjs.ojp.usdoj.gov/index.cfm?ty=pbdetail&iid=1763

Sappenfield, M. (2002, March 29). Mounting evidence links TV viewing to violence. *The Christian Science Monitor, 4.*

Sax, L. (2005). *Why gender matters.* New York, NY: Doubleday.

Sax, L. (2009). *Boys adrift: The five factors driving the growing epidemic of unmotivated boys and underachieving young men.* New York, NY: Basic Books.

Social networking fact sheet. (2015). Retrieved from http://www.pewinternet.org/fact-sheets/social-networking-fact-sheet/

Survey of inmates in state and federal correctional facilities. (n.d.) Retrieved from http://www.icpsr.umich.edu/NACJD/sisfcf/

Thompson, M. P., Kingree, J. B., & Desai, S. (2004). Gender differences in long-term health consequences of physical abuse of children: Data from a nationally representative survey. *American Journal of Public Health, 94*(4), 599–604. Retrieved from http://www.ncbi.nlm.nih.gov/pmc/articles/PMC1448305/

Veronda, R. G. (2001). *No more turning away: A revolution in education—solutions for a violent society.* San Carlos, CA: Author.

Weiner, C. (2001). *Preparing for success.* Youngtown, AZ: ECL.

West, H. C., & Sabol, W. J. (2009). Prison inmates at midyear 2008: Statistical tables. Bureau of Justice Statistics NCJ 225619. Retrieved from http://bjs.ojp.usdoj.gov/content/pub/pdf/pim08st.pdf

Wilcox, G. (n.d.). The feelings wheel. Retrieved from http://guidance.blairschools.dps.schoolfusion.us/modules/locker/files/get_group_file.phtml?fid=3367553&gid=921013&sessionid=4b45fece736991f5f6e6659cbd1fea2a

Willoughby, W. E. (2002). *Bullying among Hispanic ninth grade students.* Nacogdoches, TX: Stephen F. Austin State University.

Wireless quick facts. (2013). Retrieved from http://www.ctia.org/your-wireless-life/how-wireless-works/wireless-quick-facts

Wiseman, R. (2014). *Masterminds and wingmen: Helping our boys cope with schoolyard power, locker-room tests, girlfriends, and the new rules of boy world.* New York, NY: Harmony.

YouTube. (2015). Statistics. Retrieved from https://www.youtube.com/yt/press/statistics.html

The late Paul D. Slocumb, Ed.D. began writing and consulting on the needs of students from poverty in 1997, building on more than 40 years as a professional educator.

Throughout his career Dr. Slocumb had the opportunity to work with students and families from a wide variety of backgrounds. After addressing curricular and instructional issues for more than 30 years of his professional career, he began observing and working more directly with the academic, social, and emotional issues of boys. These experiences came together in the popular *Boys in Crisis*, now in its fourth edition. Dr. Slocumb also wrote another book on boys, co-authored with Dr. Ruby K. Payne, titled *Boys in Poverty: A Framework for Understanding Dropout*, published in 2011 by Solution Tree Press and honored with a distinguished achievement award by the Association of Educational Publishers.

Slocumb also co-authored *Removing the Mask: How to Identify and Develop Giftedness in Students from Poverty* with Dr. Payne, which was honored by an Independent Publishers Gold Award for Education in 2011. Slocumb served as president of the Texas Association for the Gifted and Talented.

Slocumb received his B.A. from the University of Houston – University Park. He earned a master's degree from Sam Houston University and a doctorate from the University of Houston – University Park.

To book a workshop or speaking engagement
on Boys in Crisis, please contact:

aha! Process, Inc.
(800) 424-9484 or
(281) 426-5300

www.ahaprocess.com